EARLY EASTERN CHRISTIANITY

EARLY EASTERN CHRISTIANITY

ST. MARGARET'S LECTURES

1904

ON THE SYRIAC-SPEAKING CHURCH

BY

F. CRAWFORD BURKITT
LECTURER IN PALÆOGRAPHY IN THE UNIVERSITY OF CAMBRIDGE

Wipf & Stock
PUBLISHERS
Eugene, Oregon

Wipf and Stock Publishers
199 W 8th Ave, Suite 3
Eugene, OR 97401

Early Eastern Christianity
St. Margaret's Lectures, 1904, on the Syriac-Speaking Church
By Burkitt, F. Crawford
ISBN: 1-59752-161-2
Publication date 4/25/2005
Previously published by E. P. Dutton and Company, 1904

TO THE MEMORY OF

WILLIAM CURETON, D.D.,

CANON OF WESTMINSTER FROM 1849 TO 1864
AND RECTOR OF S. MARGARET'S

THIS BOOK IS DEDICATED

PREFACE

"EARLY EASTERN CHRISTIANITY," the title which I have given to these six Lectures, may possibly be held to be a misleading name. My Lectures are an attempt to sketch the leading characteristics of the ancient Church of Edessa and the Euphrates Valley from the earliest times to the Council of Chalcedon. The "Eastern Church" in popular usage generally means something geographically wider. We think of Greeks and Russians, of Alexandria and Constantinople. As compared with the Church about which I have written these names belong to the West, to the great Church within the Roman Empire. It is the unique distinction of the Church of the Euphrates Valley, that alone among the developments of Christianity in the ante-Nicene age it had some of its roots in a realm outside the Roman Empire, and that the language of its learning and its aspirations was a tongue akin to that of Palestine.

It would have been possible to trace out some

of those elements in the Græco-Roman Church which were most akin to the ideas and practices which flourished at Edessa. To name but one notable example, it would be extremely interesting to compare in detail the theological and ethical standpoint of the newly discovered *Acts of Paul* with that of Serapion of Antioch and his disciple Palût. But apart from considerations of space it seemed to me better to let Syriac Christianity speak for itself. It is a far-away tale of a vanished civilisation, but an excursion into this remote region may give us a new point of view from which to look at our own ideals and beliefs.

It only remains to say that the photographs of Edessa in this volume were very kindly taken for me by Fr. Raphael of the Capuchin Mission at Urfa. The two great Columns in the Frontispiece were set up in the days of paganism, and fragments of their Dedication Inscription are still legible upon one of them. Below this may be seen a few letters containing the Moslem profession of faith cut in an early Arabic character. Between the period covered by these two Inscriptions must be placed the rise of Christianity in Edessa and its slow decline.

CONTENTS.

		PAGE
I.	THE EARLY BISHOPS OF EDESSA	1
II.	THE BIBLE IN SYRIAC	39
III.	EARLY SYRIAC THEOLOGY	79
IV.	MARRIAGE AND THE SACRAMENTS	118
V.	BARDAISAN AND HIS DISCIPLES	155
VI.	THE ACTS OF JUDAS THOMAS AND THE HYMN OF THE SOUL	193

LIST OF ILLUSTRATIONS

THE TWO GREAT COLUMNS ON THE CITADEL
    OF EDESSA . . . . . . *Frontispiece*
      The view taken looks very nearly N.E.

EDESSA . . . . *To face page* 39
      View looking S.S.W.

EDESSA . . . . ,, ,, 79
  *View looking W.S.W., with the Citadel of Abgar
and the two great Columns in the background.
The hill on the right was where Shamôna and
Gûria were martyred* A.D. 297.

EDESSA . . . . ,, ,, 155
      View looking W.N.W.

EDESSA . . . . ,, ,, 193
      View looking N.N.W.

" S. Chrysostome *that lived in* S. Hieromes *time, giveth evidence with him:* The doctrine of S. John (*saith he*) did not in such sort (*as the Philosophers did*) vanish away : but the Syrians, Egyptians, Indians, Persians, Ethiopians, and infinite other nations being barbarous people, translated it into their (mother) tongue, and have learned to be (true) Philosophers, *he meaneth Christians.*"

—Preface to the Authorised Version, *ante med.*

LECTURE I

THE EARLY BISHOPS OF EDESSA

WHEN I was asked by Canon Henson to deliver the S. Margaret's Lectures for 1904 upon the early history of the Syriac-speaking Church, I quite understood that what was required would be something rather different from a regular academical course. The study of antiquity is a fascinating pursuit to the student, but the great mass of Englishmen are not students, nor do they wish to become students. Most of us have something else to do, and time is limited for all of us. We have no time to follow the expert in his investigations, and very little even to listen to the declaration of the results which he has attained when his investigations are ended. This is the case, not because we wish to belittle the value of the study of antiquity in general or of oriental antiquity in particular, but because there is so much demanding our attention which is nearer in time and place. I feel, therefore, that I must begin by giving some reasons why any one beyond professed students should give their attention at all to this comparatively out-of-the-way subject.

The historical method of studying our religion, as opposed to the philosophical method, needs little defence, at least to those who belong to the Church of England. The Christianity we profess is not a formal theory but an organic growth, the result of a long historical process. The appeal to the "continuity of the Church" and the "historic episcopate"—to name two familiar catchwords—is a witness to the importance of a historical presentation of Anglican Christianity. In other words, the well-instructed Christian ought to have a clear general view of the development of the organisation of which he is a member.

The controversies which at various times have agitated the Church sometimes appear after the lapse of ages to be battles of words and names. Neither the orthodox nor the heterodox party seem at first to be fighting for the great questions which interest us. When we study more carefully we learn, as it were, the language of the controversy, we gain an insight into the principles at stake, and in very many cases we see that the orthodox side was fighting for the cause of real progress. I do not mean that they were fighting for the "Rights of Man" or the principles of the Constitution of the United States of America, or for any of the platforms which at present are advocated by any existing party. But given the conditions of the time, the orthodox decision was generally the solution which made the development of the Church possible, and protected it best from the ever-recurring danger of relapse into heathenism. Thus it may be argued, with very great probability, that Arianism meant the re-introduction of the Pantheon and the Hierarchy of the Gods into the official religion of the Empire, that the various forms of Gnosticism practically involved the denial of the real humanity of our Lord, that the struggle of the Church with Montanism was the fight of Order against Anarchy, and, to come to a later time, that the development of the mediæval Papacy was necessary to keep the Church together in the face of the disintegrating effects of the barbarian conquests.

Yet this way of looking at Church History is not quite satisfactory. It is not really scientific, because it is not experimental. We only know, as a matter of fact, how the Church did develop upon the one line. What would have happened had the Church become Arian or Sabellian or Montanist we do not know. It is all a matter for conjecture, because it did not really happen.

We can, it is true, compare the development of those parts of Western Christendom which split off into separate organic life at the time of the Reformation with the development of that portion which remained obedient to Rome. But this is altogether too late for our purpose. Moreover, the Catholic may always say that these separated bodies, whatever sacramental graces they may have carried off with them, are schismatics, separated from the true Body of Christ.

The Church we are about to consider in these Lectures is not open to any of these strictures. It believed itself to have had an apostolic origin, and the great Church within the Roman Empire admitted the claim. It was in full communion with all the chief centres of Christianity. The Saints of the Syriac-speaking Church are Saints of the Church universal, so far as their fame reached the West. Nevertheless there is a real difference between the Church of Edessa and the Church of Antioch and of Rome. They were divided by one of the greatest of all divisions between man and man—the barrier of language. During the years we shall chiefly consider this barrier simply acted as a partition, as a dividing-line. It did not estrange the Syriac-speaking Christians from their brethren over the border, but it separated them, so that the Church of which they were members grew up to some extent under influences different from those which helped to mould the Græco-Roman Church of the Empire.

In this lies the importance for us of Early Syriac-speaking Christianity. It is the nearest thing we can get to an experiment in Church History, to a history of the Church as it might have been, had its environment been different. We shall not expect therefore that the value of our study will consist chiefly in noting improvements in the fabric of our own Church which we can adopt from the Syrians. Such direct importations are not likely to fit themselves organically into our Western conditions of life and thought, though here and there hints for the Indian Churchman may, perhaps, be stored up. I would rather suggest that our study will help us to modify our view of the ancient Church. We shall learn how difficult it is to apply the test *quod semper, quod ubique, quod ab omnibus*. We shall learn that it was possible for an orthodox Christianity to grow up, which had in some respects a different theory of the Christian community and of social life from that which prevailed in the West. We shall learn, above all, the great lesson that a living Christianity is not tied down to a set of forms imposed from without. The century that saw Syriac-speaking Christendom unified in externals with the West by men who saw the power and the influence of external unity, saw also the permanent dismemberment of that branch of the Church into dissenting and hostile sects. I trust that what are called "our unhappy divisions" may never be healed over in this unreal fashion.

The early history of the Syriac-speaking Church is to a certain extent a matter of conjecture and inference. The historical sources are scanty, and most of the accounts of the earlier periods that we possess are compilations in which at least two inconsistent historical traditions have been blended. But if we are to understand the Syriac Christianity of the fourth and fifth centuries, we ought to have some idea of the early development of the Church in Edessa, the first centre of Christianity in the Syriac-speaking world.

Edessa was the capital of a small principality east of the Euphrates. The town had been refounded by the Greeks and called by them Edessa, but the Aramaic-speaking inhabitants of the place continued to call it Urhâi, a name of uncertain meaning, from which the Greeks formed Osrhoene (or Orrhoene) for the name of the district, and from which comes the modern name Urfa for the town. It lies on one of the great trade routes to the East, that, namely, which passes between the great Syrian desert on the South and the mountains of Armenia on the North. The inhabitants of the city and the district spoke a dialect of Aramaic akin to, but not identical with, that spoken in Palestine by our Lord and His apostles. The town must have been a centre of literary culture long before the coming of Christianity to it, and the earliest surviving writings have an ease and fluidity which seem to reflect traces of Greek influence.

The princes of Osrhoene appear to have had Arab blood in their veins, as was the case with most of the rulers of the little states on the eastern borders of the Roman Empire. A familiar instance is Aretas of Damascus, mentioned by S. Paul, whose name is spelt *Hâritha* by his fellow-countrymen. Similarly, we find among the princes of Edessa names which are almost certainly of Arab origin, like Maz'ûr and Wâ'el, and probably this is the case also with Abgar and Ma'nu. These were the favourite names among the Edessene princes; out of the whole thirty, eleven were called Abgar and nine Ma'nu.

It is not quite certain what the names really mean.

The external history of Edessa follows the usual fortunes of a border state. The realm that had belonged to the House of Seleucus was divided between the Romans and the Parthians, and Osrhoene lay on the frontier. Until the end of the second century of our era Edessa was outside the Roman Empire, and consequently within the Parthian suzerainty. In the wars of Trajan it suffered severely, being stormed and sacked by the Roman general, Lusius Quietus.[1] This took place in the August of 116. For a time the state kept its independence, but the end was inevitable. "The feeble sovereigns of Osrhoene," to quote the words of Gibbon, "placed on the dangerous verge of two contending empires, were attached from inclination to the Parthian cause; but the superior power of Rome exacted from them a reluctant homage, which is still attested by their medals. After the conclusion of the Parthian war under Marcus, it was judged prudent to secure some substantial pledges of their doubtful fidelity. Forts were constructed in several parts of the country, and a Roman garrison was fixed in

---

[1] Dion Cassius lxviii 30 (*ap. Xiphilin*): Λούσιος δὲ . . . τὴν Νίσιβιν ἀνέλαβε, τήν τε Ἔδεσσαν ἐξεπολιόρκησε καὶ διέφθειρε καὶ ἐνέπρησεν.

the strong town of Nisibis. During the troubles that followed the death of Commodus, the princes of Osrhoene attempted to shake off the yoke; but the stern policy of Severus confirmed their independence, and the perfidy of Caracalla completed the easy conquest. Abgarus [*i.e.* Abgar IX], the last King of Edessa, was sent in chains to Rome, his dominions reduced into a province, and his capital dignified with the rank of colony; and thus the Romans, about ten years before the fall of the Parthian monarchy, obtained a firm and permanent establishment beyond the Euphrates."[1]

The Romans took possession of Edessa in 216 A.D., just a hundred years after the city had been sacked and burnt by Lusius Quietus. It is during that hundred years that Christianity was planted in Edessa, and if I have delayed somewhat over matters of profane history it is in the belief that it is essential for us to study the early history of Syriac-speaking Christianity with a clear perception of the general course of events during this period. It will enable us to estimate the true historical value of the legends about the foundation of the Church in Edessa, and, at the same time, it will help to explain some of the features which distinguish

[1] Gibbon i 207 f.

the Christianity of the Euphrates Valley from the Christianity of the Mediterranean cities.

The establishment of a Christian community at Edessa is an event of real importance in the history of the Church. Edessa was the only centre of early Christian life where the language of the Christian community was other than Greek. Christianity, the child of Judaism, was nursed by the Greek civilisation of the Roman Empire, for the primitive Semitic Christianity of Palestine came to an end in the great catastrophe of the Jewish War. Christianity survived among the Greek-speaking population of the great towns of the Levant and the Ægean, and in cosmopolitan Rome. The Church of Antioch in Syria, one of the oldest of these communities, was, so far as we know, wholly Greek. The country districts, where there was a Semitic-speaking population, seem to have remained unevangelised. Where the Jews had settled the new Jewish Heresy followed, but the countryside remained pagan.

When Christianity took root in Edessa, a Syriac-speaking city with a native dynasty and culture, the whole atmosphere was different. The Syriac language was used in place of Greek, and the Church developed a national spirit. It was not long before Edessa claimed the special protection of our Lord. It was believed that the city had been evangelised by Addai, one of the seventy-two disciples, that he had been sent there from Palestine in response to a letter from King Abgar to our Lord: nay more, that our Lord Himself had answered Abgar with a promise that Edessa should be blessed, and that no enemy should ever have dominion over it.

The story of Addai and King Abgar was received by Eusebius and incorporated into his *Ecclesiastical History*. It is intimately connected with the various legends of the finding of the True Cross and of the True Likeness of Christ, and its reception forms a curious chapter in the history of human credulity. But this legend, as contained in the book called the *Doctrine of Addai*, is also a source of real value for the historian. Undoubtedly it grew up at Edessa itself, attaining its present shape by the end of the fourth century, or at any rate before the reforms of Rabbûla. The author's chronology is faulty, and his grasp of history, secular and ecclesiastical, is feeble. But he knew the place he is describing. The memory of the reign of native princes was still fresh when he wrote, and the names of his personages are genuine survivals of the ancient pagan nomenclature. Moreover he is comparatively so near to the events that his narrative contains unassimilated fragments from an older, more historical, account of the rise of Christianity in Edessa. These fragments fit in badly enough into the main story, but for that very reason we may be sure that they were not invented by the author of the *Doctrine of Addai*.

Let me put before you the general outlines of this ancient tale. Abgar Ukkâma—that is, Abgar the Black, who died in 50 A.D. after a long reign—sent an embassy to Sabinus, the deputy of the Emperor Tiberius, at Eleutheropolis in Palestine. We may remark in passing that Eleutheropolis was first so called by Septimius Severus in the year 200 A.D., and that its importance as a centre of government dates from that period. The nobles Mariyabh and Shamshagram, who with a notary called Hannan comprise the embassy of Abgar, pass over against Jerusalem on their way home and hear from travellers of the fame of Jesus the Messiah. They decide to go themselves to Jerusalem, and "when they had entered Jerusalem, they saw the Messiah and rejoiced with the multitudes who were joined to Him, and they saw also the Jews standing in groups and considering what they should do to Him, for they were disturbed to see a number of their people confessing Him. And they were there in Jerusalem ten days, and Hannan the notary wrote down everything which he saw that the Messiah did."[1] So they returned to King Abgar, and when Abgar heard he wished to go himself to Palestine, but was afraid to pass through the Roman dominions. He therefore sent a letter to Jesus by the hand of Hannan the notary, and Hannan found Jesus in the house of Gamaliel, the chief of the Jews. The letter, which begins "Abgar Ukkâma to Jesus the Good Physician"[2] declares that Abgar has come to the conclusion either that Jesus is God come down from heaven or that He is the Son of God, and goes on to invite Him to come to Edessa, to live there, and to cure the disease from which he, Abgar, is suffering.

When Jesus received this letter, He replied to Hannan the notary: "Go and say to thy Lord that sent thee unto me 'Happy art thou, that

---

[1] *Doctrine of Addai*, p. 2 f.

[2] "Good Physician" is the reading of the Syriac (p. 4), but in Eusebius (*HE* i 13) and on the ancient lintel at Ephesus we find "Good Saviour." This passage of the *Doctrine of Addai* appears to be the earliest instance in which the title Good Physician is given to our Lord.

though thou hast not seen me, thou hast believed in me; for it is written of me that they which see me will not believe in me, and they which see me not—they will believe in me. Now as to what thou hast written to me, that I should come unto thee,—that for which I was sent hither hath now come to an end, and I go up unto my Father that sent me; but when I have gone up unto Him, I will send thee one of my disciples, that whatever disease thou hast he may heal and cure. And all that are with thee he shall turn to life eternal, and thy town shall be blessed and no enemy again shall have dominion over it for ever.'"

Such is the famous letter of Christ to Abgar. It had a curious after-history. The story seems very early to have been translated into Greek, and the whole letter, with the significant exception of the last clauses, was inserted by Eusebius into his great *Ecclesiastical History*. Eusebius knew the actual course of events too well to allow the promise of the impregnability of Edessa to stand in his book. So learned a historian could not forget the sack of Edessa by Lusius Quietus under Trajan, and the absorption of the province of Osrhoene into the Empire a hundred years later. The whole correspondence is very properly branded as apocryphal in the fifth century Gelasian decree. But it had enjoyed, and indeed still continued to enjoy, a great popularity. The Bodleian possesses some fragments of Greek papyrus, dating from the fourth or fifth century, which contained it, and three years ago a lintel was found at Ephesus with the letters of Abgar to Christ and Christ to Abgar inscribed on it in Greek characters almost contemporary with Eusebius himself;[1] both these documents give the promise to the city of Abgar. The letter of Christ was regarded as a charm, and pious folk in England in the time of the Heptarchy still copied it out and wore it for a preservative "against lightning and hail and perils by sea and land, by day and by night and in dark places."[2]

To return to the *Doctrine of Addai*. After receiving the message to King Abgar, Hannan the notary painted a likeness of our Lord "in choice colours" and brought it to Edessa, where Abgar set it in a place of honour.[3] At a later period this portrait was the subject of many wonderful tales: it was believed to have been

---

[1] See the *Daily Express* for May 2, 1900.
[2] See B. M. Royal 2 A xx, *fol.* 12, printed in Dom Kuypers's *Book of Cerne*, p. 205.
[3] *Doctrine of Addai*, p. 5.

miraculously painted without human hands, and it is intimately connected with the well-known tale of Veronica. But these developments belong to a further stage of legend, and the *Doctrine of Addai* goes on at once to tell us how after the Ascension the apostle Judas Thomas sent Addai, one of the seventy-two, to King Abgar. We may pass rapidly over the greater part of the preaching of Addai, but certain details demand our attention here. When Addai comes to Edessa he lodges at the house of Tobias, son of one Tobias a Palestinian Jew, who introduces Addai to Abgar.[1] Of course Abgar is immediately healed and converted to Christianity, with large numbers of his subjects, amongst whom were a merchant community of Jews.[2] The Jews of Palestine who crucified our Lord are naturally held up to obloquy, but it is remarkable that the Jews of Edessa are represented as friendly to the new teaching.

The religion of Edessa, according to the *Doctrine of Addai*, was a worship of the Heavenly Bodies.[3] The references to Bel and Nebo come, I fear, from the Old Testament and

---

[1] *Doctrine of Addai*, p. 6.
[2] *Ibid.*, p. 32 f.
[3] *Ibid.*, p. 24 f.

not from historical reminiscence, but we may accept the statement that the people of Mabbog-Hierapolis worshipped Tar'atha, and that the people of Harran worshipped a deity called Bath Nikal. Quite lately Dr Rendel Harris has collected some striking evidence to prove that heathen Edessa was especially devoted to the Heavenly Twins, and that it is in their honour that stars appear upon the Edessene coinage. The *Doctrine of Addai* does not, however, directly speak of the Twins, but it mentions the worship of the Sun and the Moon and Venus, and of the influence believed to be exerted by the signs of the Zodiac generally. It is also remarkable that the *Doctrine* makes no reference to the two great columns on the citadel which still form so striking a feature in the Urfa of to-day.

The passages which speak about the early Syriac Canon of the Old and New Testaments, and about the manner of life practised by the converts, we shall consider in subsequent lectures. But for the main question we are now considering, the question of the general course of the history of the Edessene Church, the most important part of the *Doctrine* is its conclusion. We are told, in itself a remarkable statement, that Addai died in peace and honour during the lifetime of the believing King Abgar, and that he was succeeded by his disciple Aggai.[1] Some very late authorities make Addai gain the honour of martyrdom, but the peaceful end here given to him is one of the indications that a real historical element is contained in our main document. Aggai, on the other hand, was martyred. Ma'nu, one of the sons of Abgar, was an unbeliever, and when Aggai refused to make him a heathen diadem, such as in old days he had made for Abgar his father, this Ma'nu sent and broke Aggai's legs as he was sitting in the Church. So Aggai died, and was buried in the Church between the places for the men and for the women. And because he died thus suddenly he had no time to ordain his successor Palût, so that Palût was obliged to go to Antioch for ordination, where he was ordained by Serapion, Bishop of Antioch.

Here is an evident anachronism, an anachronism so glaring that it must be more than a mere mistake. Serapion of Antioch is a personage known to us from the *Ecclesiastical History* of Eusebius as an orthodox writer and a champion of the Four Canonical Gospels, as strict as was S. Irenaeus, his contemporary. Serapion became Bishop of Antioch in the year

---
[1] *Doctrine of Addai*, p. 46 f.

190 and held the See for about twenty-one years. If, therefore, Serapion ordained Palût, Palût could not have been converted to Christianity by one of the seventy-two Disciples, nor could the King Abgar, in whose reign he lived, have been contemporary with our Lord.

We are thus confronted in the *Doctrine of Addai* with two theories of the rise of Christianity in Edessa. On the one theory, which is that maintained in the body of the work, Christianity was planted there in the first century of our era: on the other, which is that of the epilogue, the third president of the Christian Society at Edessa was not ordained bishop till about 200 A.D., and Christianity itself cannot have reached the district much before the middle of the second century.

The story of the *Doctrine of Addai* is practically continued in a pair of documents called the *Acts of Sharbêl* and the *Martyrdom of Barsamya*. Barsamya is mentioned in the *Doctrine of Addai*,[1] and we learn that he became Bishop of Edessa in succession to 'Abshelama who succeeded Palût.[2] Barsamya, the Christian bishop, converts Sharbêl, the chief priest of Bel

---
[1] *Doctrine of Addai*, p. 33.
[2] Cureton's *Ancient Syriac Documents*, p. 71.

and Nebo : Sharbêl and Barsamya are both arrested, and the former, after cruel tortures, is put to death. Barsamya is about to undergo the same fate, when a decree of toleration arrives from the Emperors (*sic*), and he is dismissed in peace. In the *Martyrdom of Barsamya* we find again the statement that Palût was ordained by Serapion, and in accordance with this we are told that Barsamya lived in the days of Pope Fabian I., who was martyred in A.D. 250 during the Decian persecution.[1] But elsewhere in these documents the Emperor is called Trajan, and the persecuting judge who appears as supreme ruler in Edessa is called Lysania or Lusianus, although a heathen King Abgar is also mentioned.[2] The view that makes Trajan the persecuting Emperor prevailed in later times, and so the late chronicler Michael the Syrian, Jacobite Patriarch of Antioch in the twelfth century, assigns the martyrdom of Sharbêl and Barsamya to his reign.[3] Yet even Michael introduces an inconsistency, for he adds that at the same time Euphemia of Chalcedon suffered martyrdom, an event which took place in 307 during the Diocletian persecution. It

---

[1] Cureton's *Ancient Syriac Documents*, pp. 61, 71.
[2] *Ibid.*, p. 42.
[3] J. B. Chabot, *Michel le Syrien*, p. 175 b.

THE EARLY MARTYRDOMS

will be well to bear in mind this glaring anachronism when we come to Michael's account of Bardaisan.

The details of the story of Sharbêl and Barsamya do not commend themselves as historical on a close survey. Sharbêl, the converted heathen priest, not only reviles the (Greek) gods of paganism after the manner of professional Christian Apologists, but also quotes the Psalms and the Prophets as if he had been long familiar with the Scriptures. The tortures to which he is put are absurdly severe, but they are utterly unable to prevent him from haranguing the judge with considerable prolixity. Finally we are told that the persecution ceased because of the earthquakes which took place at Rome when the exiled Christians were taking away with them the bones of S. Peter and S. Paul. When the people of Rome saw the earthquake, they besought the Christians to stay; so the earthquake ceased, and they all, both Jews and Pagans, confessed Christ.[1] It is obvious that not much reliance can be placed on a document which contains such perversions of fact.

We pass on a few years and emerge at last into the light of real history. In the ancient

---

[1] Cureton, *Ancient Syriac Documents*, p. 61.

Syriac Kalendar, edited by Dr Wright from a MS. written in the year 411, we find on the 15th of November the commemoration of Shamôna and Guria, and on the 2nd of September the commemoration of Habbîb the Deacon. This ancient Kalendar, or rather Martyrology, knows nothing of Sharbêl and Barsamya, or of Aggai, a circumstance which tends to show that the cult of these early martyrs at Edessa did not rest on continuous historical tradition. It is different with Shamôna, Guria and Habbîb; their memory was never forgotten by the Syriac-speaking Church. Shamôna and Guria were beheaded at the beginning of Diocletian's persecution in 297, and Habbîb was burned alive under Licinius in 309, a couple of years before the edicts of toleration. During this period the Bishop of Edessa was named Qônâ. He died in 313, after the persecutions had come to an end, and the only act assigned to him by chroniclers is the laying of the foundations of the great Church, which was finished by his successor Sa'ad who died in 324. How Qônâ escaped during the persecution we do not know. He may have been in hiding, or possibly the governing officials may have been unwilling to arrest persons of distinction for fear of a riot. It is in any case noteworthy that he is neither praised nor blamed by the writer of the martyrdoms, himself a contemporary.

From the time of Qônâ onwards the names of the bishops of Edessa are carefully recorded in the document called the *Chronicum Edessenum*. Between Qônâ and Rabbûla the See of Edessa was held by nine bishops. Of these, Aitalâha, the successor of Sa'ad, was one of the members of the great Council of Nicæa in 325 A.D. The next but one to Aitalâha was Barses, who was exiled by the Arians. Rabbûla, who was bishop from 412 to 435, will be considered in following lectures. His episcopate is the great landmark in the history of the Syriac-speaking Church. It was while Rabbûla was bishop that the older heretics came to an end, and the new parties of Monophysites and Nestorians first became defined. In ritual and discipline also his rule marks the end of the old and the beginning of the new.

One great event in general history during the fourth century must be briefly noticed here. The invasion of Mesopotamia by the Huns from the North in the year 395 was a public calamity and is mentioned in some Christian hymns. But it had no influence on the general development of the Church, and it fell with equal force on all classes of the community. The great Persian

War belonged to a very different order of things. It has a real bearing on theology and on Church history. It lasted with intermissions from 337 to 363, and ended disastrously for the Roman cause after the defeat and death of Julian. The Empire gave up Nisibis with all the provinces beyond Osrhoene, and we can still hear in S. Ephraim's discourses echoes of the dismay with which the Christian population of the East received the disgraceful tidings. "Grief compels me to speak," he writes, "order commands me to be silent"; and I regret to say he goes on to improve the occasion by exhorting his hearers at Edessa to take warning by the fate of Nisibis, which had no doubt perished because of the thoughtlessness and luxury of its inhabitants and their immodest dancing shoes.

We should, however, obtain a very imperfect representation of the history of the Church of England if we had to re-construct it merely from published sermons. To the Christian subjects of the Sasanid monarch the war meant much more than an occasion which might be turned to good account in the pulpit. To many of them, indeed, it was literally a matter of life and death. For the Persian War of the fourth century was the first great political event in which the Church found itself taking a side. The Empire of the

Sasanids was definitely national, Persian, Zoroastrian, opposed to Christianity; and so, from the time that the Roman Empire became Christian, to be a Persian Christian was, in the eyes of the King of Kings and his government, not very different from being a Persian traitor. It was almost as difficult to be a Persian Christian under Sapor as to be a Catholic under Elizabeth, or an Anglican under Cromwell.

I do not intend to trace the rise and decay of Christianity in the Sasanid Empire. To-day I must be content with mentioning the fact of the great war and its general bearing on the theology of the Syriac-speaking Church, before going back to the outline of the earlier period. The names of bishops are the dry bones of Church History, and in making up the chain of episcopal successions we are at best only re-constructing a skeleton. But the re-construction of this skeleton is a necessary preliminary to enduing the dry bones with nerves and spirit: at least, to drop the metaphor, there is no surer way of detecting a break in the continuity of the history of a Church than by a break in the succession of its chief ministers. And it is to the great break in the succession of Edessa that I must now once more draw your attention.

What is the real meaning, we ask, of the

statement that Palût was not ordained by Aggai, but by Serapion of Antioch? The documents that make this statement, *viz.* the *Doctrine of Addai* and the *Martyrdom of Barsamya*, go on to tell us that Serapion himself was ordained by Zephyrinus of Rome, who was ordained by his predecessor, and so on up to S. Peter. The general ecclesiastical meaning is, of course, quite clear. It means that Palût was an accredited missionary of the great Church of the Roman Empire.[1] Palût was a child of Peter: no such claim is made for Addai and Aggai, his predecessors at Edessa.

But the form of the statement we are considering is curiously unhistorical. Serapion was Bishop of Antioch from 189 or 192 to 209. Zephyrinus was Bishop of Rome from 202 to 218, and certainly did not consecrate Serapion. There must be, therefore, a special reason for the mention of Zephyrinus, who was a comparatively undistinguished occupant of S. Peter's chair. I venture to suggest that this special reason is to be found in the fact that Zephyrinus was bishop at the time when Abgar IX made his famous visit to Rome. All the indications converge to show

---

[1] In the well-known words of S. Irenaeus (*Haer.* iii 1): "Ad hanc enim [sc. Romanam] ecclesiam propter potiorem principalitatem necesse est omnem conuenire ecclesiam, hoc est eos qui sunt undique fideles."

that the King Abgar who was converted to Christianity, or at least showed himself favourable to the new religion, was Abgar IX. Abgar IX. is the only ruler of Edessa who would ever have had occasion to send an embassy to Eleutheropolis in Palestine, as related in the *Doctrine of Addai*: he is said to have had Bardaisan for a friend, so that he was exposed to Christian influence; he was the only one of the later kings of his name who reigned long enough for legends to form about his personality. We need not strain our imaginations to invent an interview between the Roman Pope and the Asiatic King, but if Abgar IX were only half a Christian it is at least almost certain that his retinue would include members of the Edessene Church, who would carry back to the East, on their return, the name of the chief ecclesiastic in the capital of the world. That in sober truth a church then existed at Edessa we know from the graphic description of the great flood of 201 A.D. which is embedded in the *Edessene Chronicle*, when amongst much other damage the "Church of the Christians" was destroyed by the river Daisan.

It is, of course, possible that the intercourse between Abgar and Septimius Severus may have turned the attention of the ecclesiastics of Rome and Antioch to the Christian community of Edessa, but it is more likely that the impulse came the other way, and that Palût's career represents a movement among Syriac-speaking Christians for closer communion with the Churches of the West. We do not know, and our sources are not likely to tell us, how far Palût with his Antiochene Orders represented at the time the main stream of Edessene Christianity. Yet it is difficult to repress the suspicion that at first the Catholics, as we may call them, were in the minority. We learn from Jacob of Edessa that S. Ephraim, in a controversial homily, now lost or badly edited, complains that the orthodox are called "Palutians"; the Church, he says, ought not to be called after any man's name, but only after Christ Himself. S. Ephraim's argument, that it is the dissenting sects which are called after their founder's names, is historically accurate, but the obvious conclusion to be drawn from the name Palutian is that the Catholic Church in Edessa was a dissenting sect founded by Palût.

A somewhat similar conclusion is perhaps to be drawn from the list of prelates who have filled the office of Catholicus or Primate of the East, the head of the Church within the Persian dominions. This list is to be found in the *Book of the Bee* compiled by Solomon of El-Basra, and in one or two similar collections of historical matter. It begins with Addai. Then comes his disciple Mari; but Ambrose and Abraham, the next in order, are distinguished in the list as being "of the consecration of Antioch." Here, again, Addai is claimed as the founder of the Church, but the link is soon broken, and the succession goes back to Antioch.

One important piece of evidence remains to be considered before we sum up our historical results. The *Chronicle* of Michael the Syrian, Patriarch of the Monophysites, who died in 1199, is a compilation from various sources. The value of such a work, when it describes events which happened a thousand years before the writer's day, obviously depends on the excellence of the sources he used, and not upon his own critical judgment. For the main part of his work in the first three centuries of Christianity he is dependent on Eusebius, but for the history of Edessa he has other material. Most of it is familiar to us already; for Addai and Aggai he uses the *Doctrine of Addai*, for Barsamya and Sharbêl the heathen priest he uses the Syriac *Acta*.[1] Curiously enough, he passes over Habbîb, Shamôna and Guria, the genuine local

---
[1] Chabot's *Michel le Syrien*, p. [105] *b*.

heroes of Edessa. But in compensation he gives us the fullest biography of Bardaisan that has survived, a biography which in part, at least, must have been derived from a source considerably older than Michael himself.

He tells us[1] that in the year 154 A.D. Bardaisan was born at Edessa, where his parents had taken refuge (apparently from the Parthians), and that he was brought up at Hierapolis-Mabbog by a heathen priest. At the age of twenty-five years, *i.e.* in 179 A.D., he went to Edessa on some business, and when passing by the Church built by Addai he heard the voice of Hystasp explaining the Scriptures to the people. This Hystasp is he that succeeded to Îzâni[2] as Bishop of Edessa. Bardaisan was pleased with the discourse, and desired to be initiated into the Christian mysteries; and when the bishop heard this he taught him and baptized him and made him a deacon. Then follows some account of the astronomical and astrological heresies of Bardaisan, and at the end we are told that 'Aqai, the successor of Hystasp, having failed to convince Bardaisan of his errors, finally

---

[1] *Chabot*, p. [110] *a*. The MS. has 475 A.S. = 164 A.D., by error. The year 154 is given correctly in the much earlier and more trustworthy *Chronicum Edessenum*, and is demanded by Bardaisan's death in 222 at the age of sixty-eight.

[2] Or *Yaznai*.

anathematised him, and he died in 222 A.D. at the age of sixty-eight. "May his memory be cursed, Amen!" adds our chronicler at the end of the tale.

We shall come back to Bardaisan in a subsequent Lecture. What we must here notice is that this account supplies us with three new names of bishops of Edessa, of the succession of Addai. No other source tells us of Îzâni, of Hystasp, or of 'Aqai, and we have now to consider whether we are to accept these names, and if so, where we are to insert them in our list. Perhaps, however, the best way is first to consider whence Michael our chronicler himself took the names.

This last question resolves itself into an inquiry whether Michael's list of Edessene bishops has any independent value, or whether it be merely his own compilation from the various sources of which he has made use. For Michael, if we may accept his statements, gives us definite information. He puts Addai, Aggai and Palût in the days of the apostles; then 'Abshelama; then Barsamya in the days of Trajan; then follow Tiridat, Bozni, Shalûla, another slave; Guria, another slave; and then Îzâni, Hystasp and 'Aqai.[1] What Michael means by "another slave" I do

---
[1] *Chabot*, p. [110] *b*.

not know: the whole list is extremely confused, and no name is given between 'Aqai, who was bishop before 222 A.D., and Qônâ, who was bishop under Diocletian in 297. These confusions and imperfections make it unlikely that our chronicler Michael composed the list of Edessene bishops himself; but they do not help to commend the list to us as a serious historical document. It is noteworthy that no numbers are put before the bishops in the list, as in the lists of bishops of Rome, Antioch, Alexandria, and Jerusalem, and I venture to think that we may transpose the three names which have to do with Bardaisan to a place before Palût.

The ordination of Palût by Serapion of Antioch, which is the central fact of the Edessene succession, is passed over altogether by Michael. When we take account of this fact we see that the three bishops who come into the story of Bardaisan have been inserted far too late. The story itself mentions Addai, but Palût's name does not occur. I think we shall do best to reject Michael's order altogether. We have seen that there was some evidence to suggest that Palût, with his Antiochene consecration, occupied the position in Edessa of a dissenter from the main body of Christians. The latest tradition makes him the direct successor of Aggai; the earlier tradition makes him a disciple of Aggai, but consecrated bishop by Serapion; in actual fact he may have been a rival to the direct successor of Addai and Aggai. Bishop Hystasp, who converted Bardaisan, must have been some years senior to Palût, but 'Aqai, who anathematised the great Astrologer, seems to have been Palût's contemporary, or at most only a little his senior. Yet after all our sources know nothing of rival bishops in Edessa till the time of the Arians, and I should like to believe that the account given at the end of the *Doctrine of Addai* is in essentials true, namely, that the succession of the bishops of Edessa was broken mainly because of heathen persecution.

The early history of the Edessene Church is derived from sources for the most part unfamiliar. Much of our material is late, much of it is mixed up with unhistorical legend and fable. To give a re-construction of the history without setting the documents before you would have been unsatisfactory, while a mere quotation of the conflicting accounts which have come down to us would have led to confusion. I have therefore given you the chief *data* from the documents, with a certain amount of accompanying criticism, in order to enable you to pass judgment as to their value. I shall now go on, by way of recapitulation, to state what I conceive to have been the main outlines of that history to which our fragmentary sources bear witness.

The beginnings, then, of Christianity in Edessa started among the Jews. Christianity was first preached there by Addai, a Jew from Palestine, probably before the middle of the second century, and the first Christian community in Edessa contained a large Jewish element. At the same time the new religion came to be favourably received by some of the noble and cultivated pagan inhabitants, though it did not become the State religion till after the end of the second century. Addai died in peace at Edessa, but his successor Aggai was martyred. The Christian community, however, continued to prosper after his decease under Hystasp, for I suspect that the Îzâni of the Syriac Chronicle may be a miswriting of Aggai. Be this as it may, in the time of Hystasp the Church gained the adherence of Bardaisan, a fact which in itself shows the growing attraction of Christianity for the heathen world. Bardaisan was of noble birth, and he became a distinguished writer: it is a grave count against the Church in Edessa under 'Aqai, the successor of Hystasp, that it failed both in authority and attractiveness to retain the chief representative of Syriac philosophy within its fold. But the old order of things in Edessa about 200 A.D., both in Church and in State, was coming to an end: the State came under the dominion of the Romans, and the Church was renewed by a mission which derived its authority and its orders through the Bishop of Antioch. Palût, the new bishop, had been ordained by Serapion of Antioch, but though those outside might at first call his followers Palutians, as if they were a new sect, he or his immediate successors soon became the undisputed presidents of the Catholic Church in Edessa, and later ages remembered Palût as the disciple of Aggai himself. The followers of Bardaisan remained without the pale of the Church, and continued to the fifth century. It is not known at what time the Marcionites first established themselves in Edessa. They also remained till the time of Rabbûla, in spite of the opposition both of the Catholics and the school of Bardaisan. In Syriac, as in Greek Christian literature, we have to lament the total loss of the writings of these profoundly interesting people.

After Palût's successor 'Abshelama came Barsamya, another martyr, whom we may suppose to have suffered either under Decius or Valerian (250-260 A.D.). About thirty years later the Bishop of Edessa is called Qônâ, a personage who lived to see the end of the heathen persecutions without the disgrace of sacrificing to idols or the glory of a public confession of the Faith. But during his episcopate Edessa furnished at least three martyrs to the roll of those who suffered under Diocletian and Licinius, and the memory of their trial and execution was still fresh when the Church arrived at power and could commemorate her heroes in public. The story of Addai and the martyrdom of Barsamya are professedly taken from the public records: in other words, they were artificially composed and drawn up as learned works of history, but the author of the martyrdoms of Shamôna and Guria, and of Habbîb, speaks at least partly from personal knowledge and reminiscence. The burning fire, the terrible sea and the merciless mines are only too vividly imprinted in his memory. I think it not improbable that he was one of the guard of soldiers that accompanied Shamôna and Guria outside Edessa to the place of execution, and it was their constancy which made him from that moment a secret Christian.

I need not now continue the story of the Church in Edessa through the century of the Arian controversy. We shall hear more of the theological disputes of the fourth and fifth centuries later on. To-day we have been occupied with scaffolding. The names of bishops and the order of their succession are facts which only become of importance to us when they are intimately bound up with a knowledge of the ideas which the men represent, and when the order of the names suggests the development or the conflict of the ideas.

The early bishops of Edessa must remain to us shadowy personages. Of most of them we only know their names; and for the rest, the words that are put into their mouths in the *Doctrine of Addai* and the *Acts of Barsamya* represent the taste and the beliefs of a later age. We can do little more than repeat that the names of Addai and Aggai represent the original Christianity of Edessa, a Christianity detached in spirit from that of the Greek-speaking Christians of the Roman Empire; and that, on the other hand, with the name of Palût is associated the ideas of episcopal succession and the feeling for the unity of the Church which is symbolised by the primacy of S. Peter.

All through the history of the Syriac-speaking Church we find this double strain. Sometimes the national, independent element strikes the Western inquirer; in other departments or other times we see more prominently the effort to keep pace with the Greeks in theology, in ritual, in superstition. At last there comes a great disruption. The national elements crystallise into Nestorianism, forming a body hostile to Constantinople within the Persian dominions. For a time it had a wonderful life, and extended its missions to Samarkand and Tibet, and even to China and to Southern India. The elements more in sympathy with later Greek theology, after driving out their brethren from the Roman dominions, were themselves unable to march for long with the inspired decisions of the Byzantine Emperors. The Syrians rejected the decrees of the Council of Chalcedon, and found themselves also involved in formal heresy. When therefore the deluge came, and the barbarian followers of a new prophet overran Syria and Mesopotamia, the Christian population had little enthusiasm for the Greek dominion. The Monophysites preferred toleration under Mohammedan Caliphs to persecution under the Orthodox rule.

EDESSA.
View looking S.S.W.

[To face p. 39.

LECTURE II

THE BIBLE IN SYRIAC

The various translations of the Bible into Syriac are of the utmost interest and value to the student of Christian antiquities. In the first place, the earlier Syriac Versions are of great weight as critical "authorities," as documents by the aid of which modern scholars are enabled to re-construct the text of the Old and New Testaments in the original languages where the transmitted text is faulty, or to defend it where the transmitted text is sound. In the four Gospels especially the earliest Syriac version is one of our best authorities. But the various forms of the Bible in Syriac have a historical interest of their own apart from their critical value. They form as it were a commentary upon the history and development of the Syriac-speaking Church. The history of the Church will help us to understand and appreciate the character of the Biblical translations, and where the direct historical information is scanty the character of the Biblical translations will, to some extent, enable us to re-construct and illustrate the history.

The same thing, let us remind ourselves in passing, may be done with English Church History. We can very well illustrate the course of the English Reformation from the history of the English Bible. In Tyndale we have the Protestant reformer translating for the first time the Scriptures from the original languages into the vernacular, and in his work we catch the unmistakeable echoes of current controversies when we find the "church" appearing as the "congregation," and priests as "seniors." The various more or less official versions, culminating in the Authorised Version of 1611, mark the peculiar progress of Reformation principles in England: the irresponsible Protestant version of Tyndale was burnt by authority, but it was nevertheless used as the basis of subsequent Bibles in which the ecclesiastical vocabulary had been more or less restored.

It is unnecessary to work out the parallel in detail. The impression I wish to leave on your minds is that for studying the history of the earliest Syriac-speaking Church we are in much the same position as if we had to re-construct the course of the Reformation in England from a series of English Bibles, together with a few tales taken out of Foxe's *Book of Martyrs*. We need to use both courage and caution if our results are to be of value.

The place that is occupied among English-speaking Christians by the Authorised Version is occupied in the Syriac Churches by the Peshitta. What is known to us as the Peshitta is a Syriac version of the Canonical Scriptures of the Old and New Testaments as received by the Syriac-speaking Church. The Peshitta is the only version in ecclesiastical use. It is the Bible equally of the Nestorians, the Jacobites, the Malkites, the Maronites, and that it occupies this position is in itself proof sufficient that it is older than the latter half of the fifth century, the period when the Syriac-speaking Church began to split up into exclusive and hostile communities. The name Peshitta is not so old. The word *p'shîttâ* means "simple," and was originally applied to the current Syriac version at some period between the seventh and the ninth century to distinguish it from a revised version prepared by the Monophysite scholars, Thomas of Heraclea and Paul of Tella. This revised version was written in a pedantic semi-Greek jargon, and was provided with a complicated apparatus of critical signs embodied in the text: compared with this learned work the older translation appeared to the Syrians to be "simple." But the name Pĕshîṭtâ to denote the Syriac Vulgate is so convenient and distinctive a term that we shall do well to retain it.

The first point about the Peshitta to which I wish to draw your attention is the fixed character of its text. The range of variation found in the extant MSS. is very small, considerably smaller even than the range of variation in the MSS. of the Latin Vulgate. The variations themselves are for the most part of the most trifling description, matters of orthography, slips of writing, and such like. This is all the more noteworthy, seeing that our Peshitta MSS. date from the fifth century onwards. The whole Bible —Old and New Testaments, with the Apocrypha —is extant in Syriac MSS. of the sixth century, a state of things which cannot be paralleled in any other language but Greek, and our Greek MSS. of that age are full of startling variation from later copies.

At once some interesting problems suggest themselves. We have in the Peshitta a monument of ecclesiastical authority; what is its value? What does it tell us of the history of the Bible in the Church? What books were included in the early Syriac Canon? And what was the state of the text in those MSS. from which the translation was made?

When the New Testament in the Peshitta version was first published in the year 1555, the editor, Chancellor John Albert Widmanstätter, claimed that the Syriac of the Peshitta was the language of Palestine, the vernacular dialect used by our Lord and His apostles. This is not the case; the Syriac of the Peshitta is akin to the Aramaic of Palestine, but it is very far from being the same dialect. Syriac is the name given to the dialect of Aramaic which was spoken in the Euphrates Valley and the adjoining districts. The dialects formerly spoken in Palestine and in its neighbourhood as far north as Palmyra were also dialects of Aramaic, but distinct from Syriac. These Western Aramaic dialects differ from Syriac in the use of what may be called the article, in the conjugation and formation of the verb, and in vocabulary. The "Aramaic of Palestine" is known to us from the Aramaic portions of the Old Testament, from the Targums and other Jewish literature, from the Samaritan Liturgies and Targum, from Nabatæan and Palmyrene inscriptions; and it is not the language of the Peshitta.

It is necessary to insist on this point,

because erroneous views about the connexion of Syriac-speaking Christianity with the primitive Christianity of Palestine were formerly current, and even now are not wholly eradicated. Nothing, for instance, can be more misleading than the account of the Peshitta given in the late Dr Westcott's well-known book on the Canon of the New Testament. It is true that this work was first published so long ago as 1855, but in the 7th edition, issued in 1896, and brought up to date by a distinguished scholar, we still read "The dialect of the Peshitta, even as it stands now, represents in part at least that form of Aramaic which was current in Palestine,"[1] and "The Peshitta is the earliest monument of Catholic Christianity."[2] It is true that Dr Westcott clearly recognised that the text of the New Testament Peshitta had undergone "a decisive revision in the fourth century."[3] But stress is laid on the assumed Palestinian origin of the Peshitta, and the present Canon of the Peshitta is distinctly asserted to be that of the earliest times. Neither of these assertions are tenable in the light of the evidence we now possess.

---

[1] Ed. of 1896, p. 241.
[2] *Ibid.*, p. 250, side note.
[3] *Ibid.*, p. 242, note.

It may be as well, before we go any further, once more to remind ourselves that Antioch "in Syria" was a centre, not of Syriac-speaking culture, but of Greek culture. After Christianity became the established religion of the Roman Empire, monasteries of Syriac-speaking communities were established within or near the walls of Antioch, but it was essentially a Greek city. The condition of things in the Roman Province of Syria and the regions beyond was not very much unlike that with which we have become familiar in South Africa. Just as in South Africa the great towns are predominantly English, while nearly the whole country-side is Dutch in language and civilisation, both within and without the old political boundaries, so in Western Asia only the great cities were Greek, while the villages were peopled by Aramaic-speaking races. The importance of the establishment of Christianity in Edessa, which formed the subject of last Lecture, lies in this, that it was a Syriac-speaking city. Until a Syriac-speaking Christianity was planted in Edessa, the influence of the Church in Syria did not penetrate much beyond the Greek-speaking towns on the Mediterranean coast.

To come back to the history of the Bible in Syriac, I have already drawn your attention to the remarkable fact that our many ancient MSS. of the Peshitta all present practically the same text. Mr Gwilliam has lately edited the Gospels in the Peshitta version. He has collated over forty MSS., some of them as old as the latter half of the fifth century, and yet the variations are practically confined to questions of spelling. The text approved by ecclesiastical authority was therefore very carefully preserved in later times; is it, we ask, the original text?

It is all the more necessary to ask this question, because the magnificent series of Peshitta MSS. do not entirely occupy the field. In 1858 Dr Cureton, then Keeper of the Oriental MSS. in the British Museum, published some fragments of another Syriac translation of the Gospels from a MS. at least as ancient as any of the MSS. of the Peshitta. This translation was long called the "Curetonian Syriac," after the name of its discoverer and editor. It was evidently akin to the Peshitta, though differing in many important particulars, and the question arose which of the two more nearly represented the original Syriac translation. Cureton's MS. was very defective, but in 1893 another MS. of the same Syriac translation was discovered in the Convent of S. Catherine on Mount Sinai. This MS. is a palimpsest, *i.e.* the writing had been more or less washed out and another book written on the vellum, but the original can still in great part be made out. The Sinai Palimpsest is a very ancient MS., older even than Cureton's MS., and it differs a good deal from it both in language and in the readings of the Greek which it supports. But the two MSS. often agree in the most striking way against the Peshitta. Both MSS. describe themselves as being the *Evangeliôn da-Mĕpharrĕshê*, a title which will be discussed below.

During the last half century the controversy between the rival claims of the "Curetonian" and the Peshitta has gone on. Meanwhile evidence has been accumulating that neither the one nor the other was the form in which the Gospel was most read in early times among Syriac-speaking Christians. In original Syriac works earlier than the fifth century, as distinct from translations, the separate Gospels are never quoted by name, and the text of the quotations is generally composed of phrases taken from various Gospels. The reason of this is that the early Syriac-speaking Church used not our Four Gospels, but Tatian's *Diatessaron*. This *Diatessaron* was a harmony of our Four Gospels, made into one narrative by combining, rather than by selecting, the words of Matthew, Mark,

Luke and John. Unfortunately it fell under ecclesiastical censure, and no MS. of it in its original form has survived.

No Syriac MS. of the Acts or Epistles has yet come to light which can be supposed to preserve an earlier form of the version than the official Peshitta. There are, indeed, indications that such an earlier form did once exist, but its representatives appear to have all perished. Our knowledge of the earliest Syriac New Testament outside the Gospels has to be gathered mainly from the quotations of Aphraates and the Commentary of S. Ephraim on the Pauline Epistles. This Commentary is only extant in an Armenian translation.

The time will doubtless come when we shall be able to write the history of the Bible in Syriac as a continuous narrative arranged in chronological order. But there are still great gaps in our knowledge, and we must start from some fixed point where we have clear and trustworthy evidence about the texts current in the Syriac-speaking Church. There can be, I venture to think, very little doubt as to what that starting-point ought to be. Our oldest MSS. of the Peshitta date from about the middle of the fifth century, and the earliest piece of contemporary biography which we possess is the life of Rabbûla. Let us therefore start from the episcopate of Rabbûla, Bishop of Edessa from 411 to 435 A.D. We shall see presently that this period has special claims to be regarded as a critical point in the history of the Syriac Bible. In other matters also it forms a parting of the ways. It is the last moment when the Church in the East was nominally united. The Arians and the older heretics had been routed, while Nestorius was not yet condemned.

From 411 to 435, then, Rabbûla was Bishop of Edessa. This great ecclesiastic has not yet received from modern scholars the recognition which is his due. He was a native of Qinnesrîn ("Eagles' Nest"), a town perhaps better known to us as Chalcis in Syria; his father was a heathen priest who had sacrificed in the presence of Julian the Apostate, but his mother was a Christian. He was converted to Christianity by Eusebius, Bishop of Qinnesrîn, and Acacius, Bishop of Aleppo. After his conversion, Rabbûla went to Jerusalem and was baptized in the Jordan where Jesus had been baptized by John, and the story runs that, as the future bishop came up from the water, men saw the white sheet that covered him flash blood-red. On returning to his native place Rabbûla distributed his property to the

D

poor, freed his slaves, forsook his wife, and entrusted his little sons and daughters to convent schools. He himself went from austerity to austerity, living for a time as a hermit in the desert in the hope of being killed by the wild Arabs, and then going with his friend Eusebius to Baalbek in order to obtain the crown of martyrdom by raising a disturbance in the great Temple—somewhat after the fashion of the late Mr Kensit.[1] But the crown of martyrdom was not destined for Rabbûla, and the two enthusiasts only succeeded in getting themselves thrown down the temple steps.

These exploits hardly appeal to us, but they recommended Rabbûla in the eyes of his contemporaries, and soon afterwards he was appointed Bishop of Edessa, a post which he filled for twenty-four years till his death in 435. He was evidently a most successful ruler and organiser, a strict disciplinarian while running with the stream in the matter of doctrine. At first he seems to have sided with the Nestorians, but in the end he joined the opposite party and became the friend and correspondent of Cyril of Alexandria, whose views he supported at the

---

[1] Overbeck, *Exploits of Mar Rabbûla*, p. 196, last line. I believe his to be the earliest surviving mention of Baalbek by name; cf. Bury's *Gibbon*, v 431.

council of Edessa in 431. He even burned the writings of Theodore of Mopsuestia and earned from Nestorians the name of "the tyrant of Edessa."

Other things occupied Rabbûla's attention besides questions of religious philosophy. He was generous to the poor, kind to the sick, unremitting in personal austerity. But his importance to us is that he stands as the great enforcer of ecclesiastical order. He regulated the ritual of divine service, the discipline of the professed celibates, the customs observed by the monastic communities. And though he occupied an ambiguous position with regard to those doctrines about which the Church had not already pronounced a decision, he was unceasing in the fight against heretics and heathen. He attacked the Marcionites and the Manichees with some success, and actually persuaded the remnant of the Bardesanians to come into the orthodox fold.

Shortly after Rabbûla's death in 435 his exploits were chronicled by an enthusiastic disciple. A MS. of this work survives in the British Museum, which has been edited in Overbeck's well-known collection of ancient Syriac writings, pp. 159-210. In the course of his narrative Rabbûla's biographer has occasion to quote the New Testament several times, and each time the quotations are in marked accord with the text of the Peshitta. I need here only call attention to the phrase *lahmâ d'sungân'hôn* "bread of their need" (*Overbeck* 168₂),[1] from which it is evident that the text of the Lord's Prayer familiar to the writer agreed with the Peshitta, which has "bread of our need," and not with the old Syriac version, which has "constant bread" as its rendering of τὸν ἄρτον ἡμῶν τὸν ἐπιούσιον.

Thus at the time of Rabbûla's death, in the circle especially attached to his memory and his policy, we find the New Testament Peshitta fully established. From that time onwards the Peshitta has remained in continuous possession. The Peshitta is quoted by Syriac writers of every class, and used liturgically by every Syriac-speaking sect. The Monophysites, indeed, were not entirely satisfied, and Thomas of Heraclea, a Monophysite scholar, prepared a pedantically literal revised version, which was regarded as a critical authority and here and there actually brought into liturgical use. But even among

---

[1] The sentence runs "Grace sent them (*i.e.* Rabbûla and his companions) at sunset the bread of their need." Another clear instance of the biographer's use of the Peshitta is to be found in his quotation of Joh. i 14 (*Overbeck* 197₂₀).

Monophysites the Peshitta was never really supplanted, and the Nestorians were unswerving in their attachment to it. Besides all this, we have, as I have already told you, the testimony of a series of extant Peshitta MSS. dating from the latter half of the fifth century till after the invention of printing. All these present essentially the same type of text.

There are very few instances known to me where quotations from the Gospel in original Syriac writings later than 430 A.D. are based on versions older than the Peshitta. One of these is the pair of Gospel allusions in the romance of Julian the Apostate; in the light of other evidence it is probable that the trifling differences from the Peshitta found in these allusions are due to a reminiscence of the *Diatessaron* rather than to chance variation or a slip of memory. The other is in Jacob of Serug's still unpublished homily on the Lord's Prayer, in which he renders the petition about daily bread by "And give us the constant bread of the day" in accordance with the old Syriac rendering, and (I may add), that familiar to S. Ephraim.[1] It is, of course, in the text of the Lord's Prayer that we may expect to find the last traces of older versions: in this

---
[1] See *Lamy* iii 53.

very passage the Roman Church has retained the *panem cotidianum* of the Old Latin in her liturgy, although the Vulgate text of Matt. vi 11 has *panem supersubstantialem.*

When we work backwards from the episcopate of Rabbûla we find a wholly different state of things. The direct evidence of MSS. here fails us, for it is doubtful whether any surviving Biblical MS. can be placed in the fourth century. I am inclined to believe that the Sinai Palimpsest MS. of the Gospels is as old as the fourth century, but the MS. is not dated, and the evidence therefore is wholly palæographical and so open to some doubt. On the other hand, there is a considerable body of patristic evidence in Syriac older than 400 A.D. We have the *Acts of Judas Thomas*, the *Doctrine of Addai*, the *Edessene Canons* published by Cureton, the *Homilies of Aphraates*, the *Homilies of Cyrillona*, and last but by no means least, the genuine works of S. Ephraim. All these make up a very considerable body of writing, and many quotations from the Old and New Testaments are found in them. But while the quotations from the Old Testament agree very largely with the text of the Peshitta Old Testament, the quotations from the New Testament do not agree with the text of the Peshitta New Testament.

Nor is this difference the result of mere carelessness of quotation, for a great majority of the quotations present marked resemblances to the texts of Cureton's MS. and the Sinai Palimpsest, the two surviving MSS. of the *Evangeliôn da - Mĕpharrĕshê*, and also to the extant fragments of the Diatessaron. I need hardly trouble you here with examples: the fact is patent to any one who will compare the quotations for themselves, and would have long ago been unquestioned if the evidence of S. Ephraim had not been misrepresented. Let me hasten to add that there is no question of denying the authenticity of works assigned to an ancient Father merely on some *à priori* ground. The works of S. Ephraim are very well preserved in ancient MSS. in London and Rome. Above 400 metrical hymns and homilies, and some 250 pages of prose, survive in volumes older than the time of the Mohammedan invasions in the seventh century. All these may be accepted without question as genuine, and it is surely enough for determining the character of the Biblical text that S. Ephraim used. But the Roman edition of S. Ephraim, which dates from the middle of the eighteenth century, included a quantity of pieces taken from late MSS. and *catenæ*, many of which are clearly the

work of authors who lived generations after
S. Ephraim's day. Indeed, some of them are
expressly assigned to other Syriac writers in
older MSS. These later writings, when they
contain quotations from Scripture, use not the
text S. Ephraim used but the current version,
and thus it appeared that S. Ephraim himself
quoted from the Peshitta. Now, when the
spurious pieces are taken away from S. Ephraim
and assigned to their rightful owners, no instance
remains where S. Ephraim is clearly using the
Peshitta, while on the other hand there are
many points of agreement in his quotations
with the *Evangeliôn da-Mĕpharrĕshê* and with
the Diatessaron. This is indeed what might
have been expected, for S. Ephraim wrote a
Commentary on the Diatessaron, but there is
no evidence to suggest that he ever made a
Commentary on the Four Gospels.

To come back to Rabbûla. Before the
episcopate of Rabbûla the quotations of Syriac
writers do not agree with the Peshitta New
Testament, and they do very largely agree
with the Diatessaron and the surviving MSS.
of the *Evangeliôn da-Mĕpharrĕshê*; after the
episcopate of Rabbûla they agree with the
Peshitta, and do not agree with the Diatessaron
and the *Evangeliôn da-Mĕpharrĕshê*. The

inference is obvious that Rabbûla had himself a chief share in the publication of the Peshitta. This inference becomes to my mind something very like a certainty when we read that at the beginning of his episcopate "he translated by the wisdom of God that was in him the New Testament from Greek into Syriac, because of its variations, exactly as it was" (*Overbeck* 172). As we have seen, he was just the man to favour such a revision, and just the man to carry it through successfully. His feeling for ecclesiastical uniformity would be shocked by variations between codex and codex, and by the marked way that such codices as Cureton's or the Sinai Palimpsest differed from the Greek text as he, Rabbûla, knew it. But above all, the use of the Diatessaron would be intolerable to one who desired to assimilate the system of the Syriac-speaking Church to the universal order. The Diatessaron was the work of a heretic; it had nothing but custom to recommend it, and elsewhere than among Syriac-speaking Christians there was no such custom in the churches of God. And who could carry through the reform so well as Rabbûla? He had no official rivals, no organised opposition to deal with; the Bardesanians, who of all folk most represented native Syriac Christianity, were actually being absorbed into the main body under Rabbûla's influence.

For these reasons, therefore, I identify the "translation" spoken of by Rabbûla's biographer with the Peshitta itself. I regard it as a revision prepared by him or under his immediate direction, and I understand the use of it to have been enforced by him during his tenure of the See of Edessa.

We must now consider some objections to this theory, objections not I think irremovable, but which certainly require to be put out of the way before the theory can be firmly established. In the first place, I can imagine that the incompleteness of the Peshitta canon might be used as an argument against dating the version so late as the time of Rabbûla. As is well known, the Apocalypse and the four shorter Catholic Epistles are not included. But these are the very books that are passed over in the quotations of S. Chrysostom and Theodoret. Moreover, the canon of the Peshitta, which includes James, 1 Peter and 1 John, is really a nearer approximation to the full Greek canon than anything that can be traced earlier in Syriac. Neither in Aphraates nor in the genuine works of S. Ephraim is there a single clear reference to any of the Catholic Epistles, and the *Doctrine of Addai* says expressly: "The Law and the Prophets and the Gospel . . . and the Epistles of Paul . . . and the Acts of the Twelve Apostles . . . These books read ye in the Church of God, and with these read not others." This is the ancient canon of the Syriac-speaking Church. The canon of the Peshitta, so far from being, in the late Bishop Westcott's unfortunate phrase, "the earliest monument of Catholic Christianity," is only a half-way stage, which represents the custom of Antioch at the beginning of the fifth century, both by what it includes and by what it leaves out.

Another objection to regarding the Peshitta as the work of Rabbûla is the acceptance of it by the Nestorians. How should the Nestorians accept a revision set forth by the "tyrant of Edessa"? This would, indeed, be a grave difficulty if in the time of Rabbûla the Nestorians had been, what they afterwards became, a definite sect of Syriac-speaking Christians. But at the epoch we are now considering, the Greek Nestorians were as prominent as those who spoke Syriac, and it was not till 449, fifteen years after the death of Rabbûla, that Nestorian doctrines were formally condemned. The pro-Nestorian school, as much as their opponents, derived their doctrine from Greek theologians, and would be as anxious as any other party to possess a translation of the Bible which agreed with the Greek. As a matter of fact very few "various readings" favour Nestorianism against its opponents, or *vice versâ*; the chief exception is Hebrews ii 9, and in that verse the variation between χωρὶς θεοῦ and χάριτι θεοῦ is actually reflected in the MSS. of the Peshitta. MSS. of Nestorian origin support χωρὶς θεοῦ in agreement with Theodore of Mopsuestia, while Jacobite MSS. have "God in His grace," a strange rendering which possibly represents χάριτι θεός.

As regards the most striking feature of difference between the Peshitta and the ancient custom of Syriac-speaking Christians, the heads of the Nestorian party were at one with Rabbûla in their anxiety to substitute the Four Gospels for the Diatessaron. Rabbûla ordered that in every Church there should be a copy of the separated Gospels, and that it should be read, while Theodoret, the partisan of Nestorius, tells us how he himself withdrew over 200 copies of the Diatessaron from circulation in his diocese, and substituted in their place the Gospels of the four Evangelists. Indeed Rabbûla's change of front with regard to the doctrine of our Lord's

Nature may have helped to spread the version that he recommended, for if the Nestorian party had been persuaded to give up the Diatessaron before Rabbûla went over to their adversaries, they would not return to its use after he left them. A body of Christians in the fifth century who had given up the Diatessaron in favour of the Four Gospels would hardly revert to their heretical Harmony. Meanwhile, Rabbûla's defection to the anti-Nestorian party (as we may call the Orthodox and the future Monophysites) must have helped to recommend his Biblical policy to these also. Clear traces of the Peshitta appear in the Biblical quotations and allusions of Isaac of Antioch, who died about 460 A.D. after a long literary career. It is, however, noteworthy that Monophysite scholars appear to have been less satisfied with the Peshitta than those of the other party. The fact that all later attempts at revision of the Syriac Bible, such as the Harclean version, were the work of Monophysites may, perhaps, be taken as an indication that they had not adopted the Peshitta so early as other divisions of Syriac-speaking Christians.

The ordinance of Rabbûla mentioned above, which commands the separate Gospels to be read, demands some attention. It runs as follows: " Let the priests and deacons take care that in all the churches there shall be a copy of the separated Gospels and that it be read." The Syriac expression here rendered "a copy of the separated Gospels," is *Evangeliôn da-Mĕpharrĕshê*, *i.e.* "The Gospel of (*or*, according to) the separated ones." What exactly is meant by *Evangeliôn da-Mĕpharrĕshê*?

It will probably be clearer, even if it be not more logical, at once to give my conclusions. I believe that *Evangeliôn da-Mĕpharrĕshê* meant the Four Gospels as opposed to the Diatessaron, but not the Four Gospels in the Curetonian version as opposed to the Peshitta. In fact, I know of no term in Syriac which was used to distinguish a copy of the Curetonian version from a copy of the Peshitta. All the places where the term *Evangeliôn da-Mĕpharrĕshê* is used can be referred back to the time when there was a conscious opposition between the two classes o Gospel MSS. in Syriac, *viz.* those which had the Gospel arranged in one continuous narrative, and those which had the Gospel arranged in four separate books. The term is equally applicable to the Peshitta and to the Curetonian as opposed to the Diatessaron, but except in Rabbûla's Canon, quoted above, it was never applied to the Peshitta, because the Peshitta at once ousted the Diatessaron. The Curetonian and the Diatessaron had lived in rivalry side by side, but in the generation that succeeded Rabbûla the Diatessaron had become a mere literary curiosity; there was no longer any more reason to speak of the separated Gospels than of the separated Epistles of S. Paul.

There is, indeed, one passage that seems at first to speak of the *Evangeliôn da-Mĕpharrĕshê* as a recension of the text in contra-distinction to the Peshitta. Barsalibi in commenting upon Matt. xxvii 16, 17, says with reference to Barabbas: "Jesus was His name, for so it is written in the *Evangeliôn da-Mĕpharrĕshê*." The Curetonian MS. is defective at this point, but Barsalibi's statement has been confirmed by the discovery of the Sinai Palimpsest. The Sinai Palimpsest has *Jesus Bar Abba*, while the Peshitta, in harmony with the ordinary text, has *Bar Abba* alone. But Barsalibi did not get his information from a collation of MSS. He was a mere compiler from earlier scholars, and this very statement is found word for word in the Lexicon of Bar Bahlul. The common source of Barsalibi and Bar Baḥlul is at present unknown; it does not appear to have been the Commentary of S. Ephraim on the Diatessaron, but it may very well date from a time when the Diatessaron was current. Now the Diatessaron contained many of the peculiarities of text which make Cureton's MS. and the Sinai Palimpsest such interesting documents, but it is a curious fact that no trace of the reading *Jesus Barabba* is found in our Diatessaron authorities. I venture, therefore, to suppose that the passage repeated by Barsalibi and by Bar Bahlul is an excerpt from some commentary on the Diatessaron, or from some discourse upon Barabbas in which the Diatessaron was used as the basis of the narrative. In this case the compiler of the note does not contrast the *Evangeliôn da-Měpharrěshê* with the Peshitta, but with the Diatessaron.

One point remains to be noticed. If my conjecture be correct that Rabbûla in ordering the use of the *Evangeliôn da-Měpharrěshê* had really in view the substitution of the Peshitta for the Diatessaron, it follows that the Diatessaron was the only serious rival that the Peshitta had to face at the time of its publication. That the "Old Syriac" version of the New Testament (if I may employ the question-begging term) had had a long and complicated literary history is proved by the extensive variation between the texts of the two surviving MSS. of the Gospels in that version. The Sinai Palimpsest and Cureton's MS. are clearly representatives of one and the same translation, but they differ in some places very widely from each other, almost as widely in fact as MSS. of the Old Latin version of the Gospels. But the Patristic evidence does not suggest that the version to which the Sinai Palimpsest and Cureton's MS. belong enjoyed a wide circulation in the Church during the fourth and fifth centuries. Whatever may have been the state of things with regard to the Acts and Epistles, about which we know little or nothing, it is evident that when Rabbûla became Bishop of Edessa the form in which the Gospel was practically known to Syriac-speaking Christians was Tatian's Harmony. This explains the success of Rabbûla's efforts, and the absence of Gospel MSS. containing the Peshitta text mixed with readings derived from the "Old Syriac." The Latin MSS. with mixed texts are descended from Old Latin MSS. corrected, but not quite thoroughly, to the official Vulgate. But you cannot correct a copy of the Diatessaron into a copy of the four Gospels. It was not a question of changing the readings, but of substituting one book for another. Wherever, therefore, the change was made, and we learn from Theodoret that the change was made wholesale, no mixture of texts took place. The Diatessaron codex was taken away, and a copy of the Peshitta was put in its place.

Meanwhile the copies of the unrevised *Evangelión da-Mĕpharrĕshê* remained where they were. The two which survive contain no liturgical marks in the margins as is generally the case with books intended for service. They are, so to speak, library volumes. To us they are inestimably precious as survivals from a previous age, relics of the time before the Syriac-speaking Church became the servile imitator of Greek Christianity. But to the contemporaries of Rabbûla, who allowed them to rest undisturbed on their shelves, they were neither recommended to be used nor condemned to be suppressed by Church authority; they were simply old-fashioned books to be left alone and forgotten. Thus it has come to pass that two MSS. of the Old Syriac Gospels have survived, while not one single copy of the once popular Syriac Diatessaron has reached the hand of modern scholars.

We may now leave the Peshitta on one side. We have seen that the establishment of the Peshitta New Testament marks the coming of a new order of things almost as definitely as the adoption of the English Bible marks the English Reformation. Now we have to peer into the dark years of the earlier period, and see whether the earlier history of the

Bible in Syriac can tell us anything of the development of the early Syriac-speaking Church. The three documents that we have to consider are the Old Testament Peshitta, the Diatessaron and the *Evangeliôn da-Mĕpharrĕshê*. What are the dates of these documents, and with what stages of development in the Syriac-speaking Church are they connected?

Of the *Evangeliôn da-Mĕpharrĕshê*, the Old Syriac version of the Four Gospels, we have two copies, *viz.* the Sinai Palimpsest and Cureton's MS. The Old Testament Peshitta is represented by many MSS., all having in essentials the same text. The Diatessaron is not represented in its original form by any surviving MS., but we can form a fairly clear idea of the character of the Gospel text from which Tatian's Harmony was compiled by collecting the quotations from it in S. Ephraim's commentary (itself only preserved in an Armenian translation) and supplementing these by the quotations in the other genuine works of S. Ephraim and the homilies of Aphraates.

One thing we do know about the Diatessaron. We know within narrow limits its date; it cannot be later than 172 or 173 A.D. Tatian, who made this Harmony from the Four Gospels, came back to his native Mesopotamia from Rome about that time, that is to say a few years before Hystasp the bishop of the Christians converted Bardaisan, according to the story we discussed in the last lecture. A few years later, according to Syriac ecclesiastical tradition, Palût is ordained Bishop of Edessa by Serapion of Antioch. Now Serapion was not only a pillar of orthodoxy: his activity, we learn from Eusebius, was especially directed towards the discouragement of the reading of rivals to the canonical Gospels. It is not likely that he would have approved of the Diatessaron, itself a substitute for the Four Gospels, and the work of a man who held heretical opinions. Our first conclusion therefore must be that we can only connect the mission of Palût with the use of Tatian's Harmony by way of opposition. It is conceivable that Palût or his successors may have sanctioned the use of the Diatessaron. It is inconceivable that Palût, as Serapion's missionary, would himself have introduced it.

But some one may say, does not the missionary work of Tatian and the subsequent use of the Diatessaron in the Syriac-speaking Church suggest an easy explanation of the rise of Christianity in the Euphrates Valley? You have shown us, it may be urged, that the legendary accounts of the evangelisation of Edessa are full of contradictions. May not Tatian himself and his companions have been the original evangelists? To carry on the work Tatian may have prepared a Syriac Harmony of the Gospels. This then was the form in which the Gospel originally reached Edessa. Palût may have brought with him the *Evangeliôn da-Mĕpharrĕshê*, the Old Syriac version of the four separate Gospels. But the Diatessaron was already endeared to Syriac-speaking Christians, and the orthodox bishops purchased the obedience of their flock by allowing the heretic's Harmony to be read in Church.

Part of this, I may say at once, I believe to be a true account of what took place. I have come to believe that the Diatessaron must have preceded the Old Syriac version of the Gospels at Edessa. Even the *Doctrine of Addai* tells us that at the preaching of Addai the people assembled day by day for the daily service and for the Old Testament and the New *of the Diatessaron*.[1] And on general grounds it is very difficult to think that a Harmony could anywhere have usurped the place of the four canonical Gospels, so late as the last quarter of the second century. The air was full of the theories which had just found formal expression in S. Irenaeus.

---

[1] *Doctrine of Addai*, p. 34.

But without going any further at present on this question, let us come back to the third document, whose origin also we must explain before we can write the literary history of the beginnings of Christianity in Edessa. The Peshitta version of the Old Testament was not revised by Rabbûla. We have argued that the New Testament Peshitta was first published in Rabbûla's time, because the quotations in Syriac writers earlier than Rabbûla do not agree with its text. The same argument proves that the Old Testament Peshitta existed long before the fifth century. The quotations of Ephraim and of Aphraates, the allusions in the *Acts of Thomas*, all agree substantially with the text as preserved in our ancient MSS. I do not say there are no variations, but they are surprisingly few in number. We are carried back to the end of the second century as the latest date to which we can assign the existing version of the Old Testament in Syriac. Thus it is at least contemporary with Palût and with Tatian, and we ask how they stand one to the other?

Here, again, part of the answer is clear. The Old Testament in Syriac cannot have been the work of Tatian. Nothing that we know about Tatian, his opinions, life, or writings, would suggest that he had any knowledge of

Hebrew. But the Old Testament in Syriac is mainly a translation direct from the Hebrew. This is one of the central facts which we have to take into account in constructing our history of the rise of Christianity in Edessa. All through the Old Testament, but especially in the Pentateuch, the Peshitta reveals itself as the handiwork of one who had a good knowledge of Hebrew, and a still more intimate acquaintance with some branches of Jewish tradition. I do not forget that the influence of the Greek Bible, especially in Isaiah, often makes itself felt; that element I shall notice later. But the main point is clear. Whatever revision the version may have received at later times, it is almost impossible to conceive the elements in the Peshitta which betray Hebrew knowledge as the work of Christian Syrians. The Old Testament Peshitta must have been, in the first instance, the work of Jews. To give but one instance out of many, what but knowledge of Jewish Aramaic nomenclature could have induced the Syriac Bible to call the land of Bashan (which the Greeks call *Batanaea*) by the name *Mathnîn*?[1] It is not likely that the good folk of Edessa had a special nomenclature for the petty districts east of the Jordan.

---

[1] *E.g.* Nahum i 4; 1 Chr. v 16, etc.

You remember that when Addai came from Palestine to Edessa, according to the story, he found there a community of trading Jews. He himself lodged with one Tobia, son of Tobia, a Jew of Palestine. According to the story, again, Addai's preaching was successful among the Jews. What does this mean, but that Edessa was a centre of Jewish life before it was a centre of Christianity, and that when Christianity came, it made, as at Corinth in S. Paul's time, many converts from among the Jewish community? Thus we may infer that the Old Testament in Syriac was originally a vernacular rendering of the Hebrew Scriptures made by Jews for Jews resident at Edessa and speaking the language of the country.

Several indications seem to me to confirm this theory. The date is appropriate. With the loss of the national life in Palestine it became increasingly necessary to give the Scriptures in the tongue of the local community. Possibly also the favour which Josephus tells us that the royal house of Adiabene displayed for some time towards the Jewish religion may have given an impulse towards translating the Law and the Prophets into the vernacular of the Euphrates Valley. The Peshitta, moreover, appears to have been used as the basis of the existing Jewish Aramaic Targum on the Book of Proverbs. But if we regard the Peshitta as a Jewish work, we must at the same time confess that we cannot claim to have the translation quite in its original form. In the Prophets it is evident that the Syriac has been here and there revised to make it agree with the Greek, *i.e.* with the Church's Bible. And here again I seem to trace the hand of Palût, or perhaps it would be more scientific here, as elsewhere, to say the mission from Antioch which is associated with the names of Palût and Serapion.

One thing I venture to think certain with regard to the Old Syriac version of the Gospels, and that is, that it was later than the Old Testament Peshitta. This is clear from the accurate way in which the Old Testament names are spelt. To go no further than Abraham, Isaac, and Jacob, it requires some antiquarian knowledge to re-transcribe into Semitic letters the Greek words Ἀβραάμ, Ἰσαάκ, Ἰακώβ. Each of these names is spelt with a different guttural in Hebrew, and the spelling is correctly preserved in the Old Testament Peshitta, as is natural in a translation from the original. But the Syriac Gospels are, of course, a translation from the Greek, and in the Greek the Semitic gutturals are unrepresented. The fact that the

Old Syriac Gospels preserve the names of the Patriarchs correctly is in itself very strong evidence that the translator of the Old Syriac Gospels was familiar with the Old Testament in Syriac.

The same argument suggests the priority of the Old Testament Peshitta to the Diatessaron, though in the Diatessaron the proper names do not appear to have been so carefully equated to their Hebrew equivalents. The mutual relations of the Old Syriac Gospels and the Diatessaron —I use the term advisedly, for the text of these works were undoubtedly modified the one from the other during their long history—their mutual relations can only be adequately discussed in detail, and textual detail is eminently unsuited to Lectures such as these. But I venture to assert that the main textual characteristics of the Diatessaron and the *Evangeliôn da-Mĕpharrĕshê*, *i.e.* the Old Syriac version of the Four Gospels, can be distinguished in a general way. The two works often agree in language in the most curious and intimate fashion. Again and again we find the Diatessaron agreeing in turns of expression or remarkable renderings with the Sinai Palimpsest or Cureton's MS. But in questions of real various readings in the underlying Greek text the agreement is not so pronounced. In text the Diatessaron agrees, much more than the Old Syriac does, with Codex Bezae and the Old Latin version. In a word, it came from the West, from Rome, and it agrees with the Western and Roman text. I have a strong suspicion that much of what is thought to be specially "Western" in the Old Syriac Gospels is derived through the Diatessaron from the text current in Rome in the middle of the second century.

As I have said, demonstration of these textual affinities is wearisome and unconvincing, except for those prepared to weigh a large mass of technical evidence, and to consider a number of the minor problems on their own merits. I shall not attempt such a demonstration here. In its place I shall venture to set before you a picture of the conclusions to which I have arrived. Such a picture cannot claim to be more than a consistent explanation of the historical data; the demonstration of its general truth, if you accept it, must be sought for in its agreement with the course of history.

First, then, we are to suppose a Jewish colony settled at Edessa, who have provided themselves with a translation of the Hebrew Scriptures, including some non-canonical writings such as the Wisdom of Ben Sira. To this colony comes a Christian missionary, Addai by name. The mission, as at Corinth, is successful. The majority of the Jews join the new movement, together with a number of the Gentile natives of the place. The date of this movement can only be conjectured. Doubtless it was later than the time of the sack of Edessa during the wars of Trajan. A likely date, I venture to think, is the period of Bar Cochba's rebellion, about 135. That period was a parting of the ways for many Jews; and those who disapproved of the policy of political revolt and of the theology of Aqiba might more likely then than at a later period accept the solution offered by the Christian religion.

The first Christian community at Edessa probably had no New Testament. The Law and the Prophets, as interpreted in the new light, sufficed for them. But about a generation after Christianity first appeared in Edessa, Tatian the philosopher, returning to end his days in his native Mesopotamia, supplied the want by publishing a Syriac translation of his Harmony of the Gospels. The circumstance that on Syriac ground it had no rivals made the Syriac Diatessaron an instant and assured success. Elsewhere it was a literary curiosity, but among Syriac-speaking Christians it was the Evangelic record. Finally, about 200 A.D., after a persecu-

tion had disorganised the Church in Edessa, it
was re-established, on the basis of closer union
with the Catholic Church inside the Roman
Empire, under Palût, a bishop who brought in a
version of the New Testament—*i.e.* the Four
Gospels, Acts, and the fourteen Pauline Epistles
—together with an edition of the Old Testament,
slightly revised from the Greek, especially in
Isaiah and the Psalms, and enlarged by versions
from the Greek of the Old Testament Apocrypha.

Palût at first was regarded by some as the
leader of a sect, but he or his immediate successors reconciled the great majority of the
Christians in Edessa and the Euphrates Valley
to the Catholic organisation. One point, however,
was yielded to custom. The Four Gospels were
received and studied by scholars, but the
Diatessaron continued to be read in Church,
and to be the form in which the Gospel was
familiarly known to Syriac-speaking Christians
down to the episcopate of Rabbûla early in
the fifth century. Rabbûla suppressed the
Diatessaron and substituted in its place a
revision of the Old Syriac version of the Four
Gospels, in which both the readings and the
renderings were brought into much closer con-
formity with the Greek text as read in Antioch
in the fifth century. At the same time, also in

accordance with the custom of Antioch early in the fifth century, he introduced a version of the First Epistle of S. Peter, the First Epistle of S. John, and the Epistle of S. James, together with a revised text of the Acts and Pauline Epistles.

The text of the Gospels underlying the Syriac Diatessaron, where it can be recovered in its original form, represents the Greek text as read in Rome about 170 A.D. The text of the Gospels in the Old Syriac version, represents, where it differs from the Diatessaron, the Greek text as read in Antioch about 200 A.D. Finally, the text of the Peshitta Gospels, where it differs from the Old Syriac and from the Diatessaron, represents the Greek text as read in Antioch about 400 A.D.

This rapid summary of conclusions is, of course, to some extent hypothetical. But I venture to claim that it has been made in accordance with what the evidence, both textual and historical, actually suggests, and I hope that the more important parts may be in the future more formally established.

EDESSA.

View looking W.S.W., with the Citadel of Abgar and the two great Columns in the background. The hill on the right was where Shamôna and Guria were martyred A.D. 297.

[To face p. 79.

LECTURE III

EARLY SYRIAC THEOLOGY

It has ever been the wisdom of the Church of England to recite on the greater Feasts of the ecclesiastical year the Latin profession of faith known to us as the Athanasian Creed. That venerable document is now unpopular. It is argumentative and unsentimental. But there is one sentence of the Athanasian Creed which puts the essence of the great controversies of the fourth and fifth centuries so tersely that I have ventured to use it as a sort of text for my discourse this afternoon. As you all know, the Athanasian Creed teaches us to say: "For like as we are compelled by the Christian verity to acknowledge every Person by himself to be God and Lord; so are we forbidden by the Catholick Religion to say, There be three Gods, or three Lords."[1]

---
[1] In the original the words are: *Quia sicut singillatim unamquamque personam et Deum et Dominum confiteri christiana ueritate compellimur, ita tres Deos aut Dominos dicere catholica religione prohibemur.*

The *Catholick Religion* is the living and continuous tradition of the doctrine once committed to the saints by revelation, the *Christian verity* is the logical development by Christian thinkers of the devotion of the faithful to their Lord, as interpreted in the light of Greek philosophy. Here at last we reach what for Christians is not necessarily sacred. It is a real and serious question, how much of the expression of our religion is conditioned not by Divine revelation, but by the effort to fit it in to the philosophical ideas current at the time when Christian theology became articulate. To-day I shall attempt to throw a sidelight on the great theological controversies by examining what was thought of some fundamental articles of the Christian religion by Syriac-speaking Churchmen who lived apart from the atmosphere of Greek and Latin thought.

We must not take the sermons in the *Doctrine of Addai* as the earliest expression of Syriac theology, for we have seen that this work contains some late elements, and it is only likely that the redactor of an apocryphal work writing at the very end of the fourth century would put into Addai's mouth phrases which were never current until they were coined in the stress of controversy. As a matter of fact, that excellent scholar the Abbé Tixeront, who has very carefully examined the theological statements in the *Doctrine of Addai*, comes to the conclusion that the phraseology is post-Nicene in thought as well as in date. But if we cannot use the *Doctrine of Addai* as a starting-point, we have an excellent substitute in the work commonly known as the *Homilies* of Aphraates. This work is admirably fitted, both from the scope of its contents and the personality of the writer, to serve as our introduction to the theology of the early Syriac-speaking Church.

Aphraates, or more accurately *Afrahaṭ*, commonly known as the Persian Sage, flourished in the first half of the fourth century. The first ten of his twenty-two Homilies were composed in the year 337, the remaining twelve in 344, and the additional Homily *On the Cluster* is dated 345 A.D. He was a monk and a bishop. One rather late tradition claims him for the head of the Convent of S. Matthew near Mosul. It is certain that he had a seat in a Synod held in the year 344, and that he was selected to draw up the encyclical letter of the Synod addressed to the Metropolitan diocese of Seleucia and Ctesiphon. This letter he subsequently published as No. 14 of the Homilies.

The plan of Aphraates' great work is

admirably fitted to give us a general survey of Syriac theology. We speak of the "Homilies" of Aphraates, but the volume of discourses which goes by this name is not a collection of occasional sermons. On the contrary, it is a full and ordered exposition of the Christian Faith in answer to a request for information from an inquirer. The twenty-two Homilies correspond to the twenty-two letters of the Semitic alphabet, and the first word of each Homily begins with the corresponding letter of the alphabet in order, the first with *Alaph*, the second with *Beth*, and so right through. This is not a mere fanciful quip, but a serious plan for preserving the true order of the discourses. It is difficult to interpolate or mutilate an acrostic without immediate discovery. And as if the acrostic arrangement were not enough, Aphraates enumerates the series in order at the end of the twenty-second Homily.

It is necessary to emphasise beforehand the official position and the unblemished repute of Aphraates, if we are to appreciate the significance of what he has to say. Later generations of Syriac writers have very little to tell us about him beyond what we learn from his writings, but all alike, both Nestorians and Monophysites, testify to the orthodoxy of this fourth century Father.

THE HOMILY ON FAITH

Let us begin with Homily I. *On Faith.*[1] Out of the abundance of the heart the mouth speaketh and in a doctrinal treatise that which is put first is in the eyes of the writer fundamental. Faith, according to Aphraates, is like a building made of various materials of various colours. But the foundation of our faith is Jesus Christ, the Rock upon which the whole is built, as said the prophets (§ 2). First, a man believes, then loves, then hopes, then is justified and perfected, and he becomes a Temple for the Messiah to dwell in, as Jeremiah said: *The Temple of the Lord, the Temple of the Lord—ye are the Temple of the Lord, if ye will make fair your ways and your works,*[2] and as said our Lord Himself *Ye are in Me, and I am in you* (§ 3). The man who has Faith will study to make himself worthy of being a dwelling-place for the Spirit of the Messiah. There must be Fasting, Prayer, Love, Alms, Humility, Virginity, Continence, Wisdom, Hospitality, Simplicity, Patience, Gentleness, Sadness,[3] Purity: Faith asks for all these

---

[1] This Homily is translated in full by Dr Gwynn, *Nicene and Post-Nicene Fathers*, vol. xiii, pp. 345-352. It has also been translated by Dr Budge in his edition of Philoxenus, vol. ii, pp. clxxv-clxxxvii. The analysis here given, together with much of the material of the present lecture, is taken out of my own little book *Early Christianity outside the Roman Empire*.

[2] Jer. vii 4, 5 (*Pesh.*).

[3] A technical term for the monastic life.

ornaments (§ 4). Christ is both the foundation and the inhabitant of the House of Faith: Jeremiah says men are the Temples of God, and the Apostles said: *The Spirit of Christ dwelleth in you.* This comes to the same thing for the Lord said: *I and my Father are one* (§ 5). The Messiah is spoken of by the prophets as a Stone or Rock (§§ 6-9), and as a Light (§§ 10-11). He is the only foundation that can stand the fire (§§ 12, 13). Such Faith the Saints of old time had (§§ 14-16), and those also who were benefited by our Lord on earth (§ 17). Faith carries us up to heaven, saves us from the Deluge, looses the prisoners, quenches the fire, feeds the hungry, brings back from the grave, stops the mouths of lions, humbles the proud, exalts the meek (§ 18).

Aphraates does not leave us in vague generalities. After the praise of Faith he goes on to define it.

"For this," he says (§ 19), "is Faith:—
> When a man shall believe in God, the Lord of all,
> > That made the heavens and the earth and the seas and all that in them is,
> > Who made Adam in His image,
> > Who gave the Law to Moses.
> > Who sent of His Spirit in the Prophets,
> > Who sent His Messiah into the world;
> And that a man should believe in the bringing to life of the dead,

And believe also in the mystery of Baptism:
This is the Faith of the Church of God.
And that a man should separate himself
from observing hours and sabbaths and months and seasons,
and enchantments and divinations and astrology and magic,
and from fornication and from revelling and from vain doctrines, the weapons of the Evil One, and from the blandishment of honeyed words, and from blasphemy and from adultery,
And that no man should bear false witness,
and that none should speak with double tongues:
These are the works of the Faith that is laid on the true Rock, which is the Messiah,
upon whom all the building doth rise."

Such is the Creed of Aphraates. To him Christianity was the revelation of a Divine Spirit dwelling in man and fighting against moral evil, not first and foremost a tissue of philosophical speculation about the nature of the Divinity in itself. But this is wholly alien to the temper of Greek and Latin Christianity, as it manifests itself from the fourth century onward.

About 150 years after Aphraates wrote, Philoxenus, Bishop of Hierapolis, a distinguished Syriac scholar and theologian, wrote his Discourses on the Christian Life and Character. He also began with Christian Faith and he also thought well to define it. This is what he says.[1] "All these things by Faith thou hast heard concerning God: that He is from everlasting and world without end, and that He existeth in His own essence, and that He hath not come into being from anything else; and that He is not One Person, but an essential substance that is believed and confessed in Three Persons. And, moreover, concerning the Persons the word of Faith teacheth thee to affirm that He Who begot hath not been divided, and that He Who was begotten hath not been separated, but the Father existeth with His Son essentially and everlastingly, together with the Holy Spirit consubstantial with Them." And so on, and so on, for as much again as I have read, followed by a disquisition upon the nature of the Cherubim, and what is of Faith concerning their spiritual constitution. In Philoxenus the Faith has ceased to vivify the whole personality; it has become a matter of the head and not of the heart, a matter of theological adhesion rather than of moral allegiance. With the Syrians, as with us, the philosophy of the Greeks was an alien mode of thought, and a Faith which expresses itself in a foreign or an outworn philosophy tends to become fundamentally artificial.

It must not be supposed that Aphraates did

---
[1] Budge's *Philoxenus* i 32 (Eng. Tr. ii 29).

not acknowledge the Trinity. We learn from him that the Syriac-speaking Church, like the rest of the Christian world, baptized in the Triple Name, and his evidence is confirmed by the *Doctrine of Addai* and other early Syriac documents. "The Head of the Man," says Aphraates (xxiii 63 = *Wright* 500), "is the Messiah. O thou that swearest by thy head and that falsely, if thou dost affirm the three great and glorious Names invoked upon thy head, the Father and the Son and the Holy Spirit, when thou didst receive the seal of thy life, in a word, if Baptism be affirmed by thee swear not by thy head!" Or again (xxiii 60 = *Wright* 496), "Above the heavens, what is there, who doth suffice to tell? Beneath the earth, what is laid, there is none to say! The firmament, upon what is it stretched out? or the heavens, upon what are they hung? The earth, on what is it pillowed? or the deep, in what is it fixed? We are of Adam, and here with our senses we perceive little. Only this we know: that God is one, and His Messiah one, and one the Spirit, and one the Faith, and one Baptism. More than thus far it does not help us to speak; if we say more we fall short, and if we investigate we are helpless." I need hardly remind you that the "investigation" which

Aphraates has in mind is speculation and empirical analogy, not the patient and humble co-ordination of ascertainable facts.

I must not omit to point out one remarkable feature of Aphraates's doctrine of the Spirit. When we speak in the Creed of "the Lord, the Giver of Life," we are obliged to assign a sex to the Holy Spirit. We have to choose between *Lord* and *Lady*. The Greek πνεῦμα is of course neuter. But in Semitic languages there is no neuter, and *Rûḥ*, the word for wind or spirit, is feminine; in the older Syriac literature, therefore, before the influence of Greek theology made itself felt, the Holy Spirit also is feminine. Thus in the old Syriac version of John xiv 26 we actually read *The Spirit, the Paraclete, she shall teach you everything*.[1] Thus it is only in accordance with the earliest usage that in a doxology (xxiii 63 = *Wright* 498) Aphraates ascribes "glory and honour to the Father and to His Son and to His Spirit, the living and holy," where *living* and *holy* are feminine adjectives in the older MS. But he goes further: it is not a question only of grammatical

---

[1] In the Peshitta *she* (or *it*) is changed to *he*. Another place where the feminine seemed too heterodox to stand is Lk. xii 12. But in many passages the feminine is retained even in the Peshitta, *e.g.* Lk. iv 1; Joh. vii 39.

nicety with Aphraates. In the treatise *On Virginity against the Jews* (xviii 10 = *Wright* 354) he says: "We have heard from the law that a man will leave his father and his mother and will cleave to his wife, and they will be one flesh; and truly a prophecy great and excellent is this. What father and mother doth he forsake that taketh a wife? This is the meaning: that when a man not yet hath taken a wife, he loveth and honoureth God his Father, and the Holy Spirit his Mother, and he hath no other love. But when a man taketh a wife he forsaketh his Father and his Mother, those namely that are signified above, and his mind is united with this world; and his mind and his heart and his thought is dragged away from God into the midst of the world, and he loveth and cherisheth it, as a man loveth the wife of his youth, and the love of her is different from that of his Father and of his Mother."

We shall come across this view of the Holy Spirit again when we consider the *Acts of Thomas*.[1] Here I must remind you that there is very early Christian authority for it. In the

---

[1] Cf. also Philoxenus's *Prologue*, p. 17 (E. Trans.), a passage which is probably an echo either of Aphraates or of the *Hymn of the Soul* itself.

ancient *Gospel according to the Hebrews*, as quoted by Origen and S. Jerome, our Lord Himself speaks of the Holy Spirit as His Mother. Origen (*in Joann.* ii 12), who is concerned to show that all things, including the Holy Spirit, came into existence through the Logos, does not reject this saying as "apocryphal," but explains it away. He argues that the Holy Spirit does the will of the Father, and therefore may rightly be described as the Mother of Christ, in accordance with Matt. xii 50. Perhaps it was inevitable that the thought of the Holy Spirit as the Queen of Heaven should be eliminated from Christian theology, but before we condemn the doctrine altogether let us remember that the theology of the age which followed its final disappearance, at the bidding of popular sentiment, by a false application of logic to Divine affairs, degraded the Christian vocabulary with the word Θεοτόκος.

To come back to Aphraates. His doctrine of the Person of Christ is also very far removed in expression from what was usual in later times. But just as Aphraates' doctrine of the Spirit is nothing new, but a survival of one of the most primitive Christian beliefs, so too Homily XVII, entitled *Of the Messiah that He is the Son of God*, is an echo of one of the most remarkable sayings in S. John's Gospel.¹ This Homily, like so many that Aphraates wrote, is directed against the Jews, who complained that Christians worshipped a man whom they called Son of God, in defiance of God's own word *I am God and there is none beside Me* (§ 1). Aphraates sets himself the task of defending the Christian practice, even if he should concede to the Jews that Jesus whom the Christians call God was only a man. "Though," he continues, "we do affirm that Jesus our Lord is God the Son of God, and the King the Son of the King, Light from Light, Son² and Counsellor and Guide and Way and Saviour and Shepherd and Gatherer and Door and Pearl and Lamp; and by many Names is He called. But now we will show that He is the Son of God, and that He is God who from God hath come" (§ 2). For the name of divinity has been given to just men, as for instance to Moses, who was made a God not to Pharaoh only but also to Aaron³ (§ 3); and though the Jews say God has no son, yet He called Israel His First-born,⁴ and Solomon His

---

[1] Joh. x 33-36. The Homily is translated in full by Dr Gwynn pp. 387-392.

[2] *Sic*: cf. Isaiah ix 6, and also § 9.

[3] Exod. vi 1; vii 1.

[4] Exod. iv 22, 23.

son.¹ David also says of them: *I have said, Ye are Gods and sons of the Highest all of you*² (§ 4). God gives the most exalted titles to whom He will: He called impious Nebuchadnezzar *King of Kings*. For man was formed by Him in His own image to be a Temple for Him to dwell in, and therefore He gives to man honours which He denies to the Sun and the Moon and the host of Heaven³ (§§ 5, 6). Man of all creatures was first conceived in God's mind,⁴ though he was not placed in the world till it was ready for him (§ 7). Why should we not worship Jesus, through whom we know God, Jesus who turned away our mind from vain superstitions and taught us to adore the One God, our Father and Maker, and to serve Him? Is it not better to do this than to worship the kings and emperors of this world, who not only are apostates themselves but drive others also to apostasy? (§ 8). Our Messiah was spoken of in the prophets even to the details of the Crucifixion (§§ 9, 10). We therefore will continue to worship before the Majesty of His Father, who has turned our worship unto Him. We call Him God, like

---

[1] 2 Sam. vii 14; cf. Heb. i 5.
[2] Ps. lxxxii (lxxxi) 6.
[3] Deut. iv 17.
[4] Ps. xc (lxxxix) 1, 2.

Moses; First-born and Son, like Israel; Jesus like Joshua, the son of Nun; Priest, like Aaron; King, like David; the great Prophet, like all the prophets; Shepherd, like the shepherds who tended and ruled Israel. And us, adds Aphraates, has He called Sons, making us His Brothers, and we have become His Friends (§§ 11, 12).

Nothing less than this full abstract does justice to Aphraates' style and method. It is surely most surprising and instructive to meet with work animated by this spirit in the middle of the fourth century. It is not exactly what we are accustomed to read in the Fathers, but it follows too closely the lines of our Lord's answer to the Jews for us to brand it as unorthodox. The Persian sage lived outside the Roman Empire and was educated in a culture but little touched by Greek philosophy. He did not feel that necessity for logical subordination, for the due relation of the parts to the whole, which the Greeks were the first of mankind to strive after.

To me, I confess, the efforts of Aphraates after a tenable Christology evokes a more sympathetic echo than the confident metaphysics of the "restless wits of the Grecians," to use the phrase of Hooker. He seems to have been aware that it is impossible for man to construct a logical scheme of the universe. But he held the two main positions of Christian belief as strongly as the author of the *Quicunque vult*. On the one hand, he was wholly penetrated by the monotheism of the "Catholick Religion"; on the other, his loyalty and devotion to his Lord assured him that no title or homage was too exalted for Christians to give to Jesus Christ, through whom they had union with the Divine Nature. It is upon the simultaneous holding of these two positions that Christian theology rests, not upon the form in which they were co-ordinated by the metaphysical science of the Græco-Roman Church.

> "The highest place that Heav'n affords
> Is His, is His by right."

This cry voices the demand of the Christian conscience; it rests with the theologians and the metaphysicians to determine how Heaven differs from Olympus or Nirvana.

The importance of Aphraates in the Christological Problem, which still, as M. Loisy has been justly reminding us, demands the serious consideration of Churchmen,[1] is that he shows

---

[1] Le Christ est Dieu pour la foi. Mais les gens nous demandent maintenant de leur expliquer Dieu et le Christ, parce que nos définitions sont conçues en partie dans une autre langue que la leur. Une traduction s'impose. Ainsi entendu, le problème christologique est encore actuel" (*Autour d'un petit Livre*, p. 155)

us that it was possible to hold the Christian position with different watchwords from those which the Church borrowed from her refractory sons Tertullian and Origen.

We come now to the personage who of all the sons of the Syriac-speaking Church is best known by name to the western world. Ephraim, commonly called Ephraem Syrus, died at Edessa in the year 373, in the reign of the Arian Emperor Valens. His earlier home had been Nisibis, where he lived until it was abandoned to the Persians in 363 by Jovian, after the defeat and death of Julian the Apostate. At Edessa Ephraim lived as an anchorite or solitary in a cell outside the city, but his fame as an expositor and as a champion against heresy was great even during his lifetime. He is said to have paid a visit to S. Basil of Cæsarea in Cappadocia, and to have been ordained by him a Deacon.

What has given S. Ephraim his magnificent reputation it is hard to say. According to his biographer he is to be accredited with the honour of having invented the Controversial Hymn, a rather melancholy addition to public worship. His interest to modern scholars arises from the fact that a Syriac writer of the fourth century, whose works are excessively voluminous and well preserved, cannot help affording us many curious glimpses into the life and thought of the Church to which he belongs. But it is a weary task, gleaning the grains of wheat among the chaff. Ephraim is extraordinarily prolix, he repeats himself again and again, and for all the immense mass of material there seems very little to take hold of. His style is as allusive and unnatural as if the thought was really deep and subtle, and yet when the thought is unravelled it is generally commonplace. Take for instance the 13th of the Nisibene Hymns, inscribed *Concerning S. Jacob and his Companions.*[1] S. Jacob, it should be premised, had been Bishop of Nisibis; he was succeeded by Babu, and Babu was succeeded by Walgesh or Vologeses, who was still alive when the poem was composed.

I.

Three illustrious Priests,
In the type of the two great Lights,
Transmitted and delivered to one another,
Throne and Hand and Flock:
To us, whose grief was great for the two,
The last was wholly consolation.
 To Thee be glory, Who didst choose them!

---

[1] Bickell's *Carmina Nisibena*, p. 20; translated by Gwynn, p. 180.

II.

He Who created the two great Lights,
Chose for Himself the three great Lights,
And set them in the three
Cloistered darknesses that came to pass.
When the pair of Lights were quenched
The last was altogether radiant.
To Thee be glory, &c.

III.

The three Priests were treasurers
Who held in their integrity
The key of the Trinity;
Three doors did they open to us,
Each one of them with his key
In his time [1] was opening his door.
To Thee be glory, &c.

IV.

With the first had been opened the door
To the war of the two hosts,
With the middle one had been opened the door
To the Kings of the two winds,
With the third had been opened the door
Of the ambassadors of the two sides.

(From this stanza the reader is supposed to learn that during the episcopate of Jacob the war broke out between the Romans from the West and the Persians on the East, that the war continued during the episcopate of Babu, and that an armistice was concluded during

---

[1] Read *b'zaβneh* instead of *bazb'zeh*.

the episcopate of Vologeses. I omit a dozen stanzas similar to those I have quoted to you and come to No. XVIII).

XVIII.

Nisibis planted on the waters,
Waters concealed and exposed!
Living founts within her,
A noble river without her!
The river outside deceived her,
The fountain within preserved her.

XIX.

The first Priest was her vine-dresser,
Her branches he increased to the heavens;
Lo, when dead and buried within her
He has become fruit in her bosom!
For all that the pruners came,
The fruit within her kept her safe.

XX.

The time of her pruning had arrived,
It entered and took away her vine-dresser,
That she should not have an intercessor;
She hasted, and in her subtlety
Laid in her bosom her vine-dresser,
That she might be delivered by her vine-dresser.

XXI.

Imitate, ye sensible ones,
Daughters of Nisibis, imitate Nisibis,
That laid a Body within her
And it became a Wall without her!
Lay in you a living Body,
That it may be a Wall for your life.

The meaning of these latter stanzas is that S. Jacob, Bishop of Nisibis, protected the city during his life by his prayers, and that, now he was dead and buried within the city, his relics were equally efficacious in keeping out the Persians.

I have quoted this specimen of the poetry of S. Ephraim, not because I think it beautiful or inspiring, but because it is eminently characteristic. Of course it sounds somewhat less bald in the original Syriac, because the original Syriac is in metre. But so far as I can see it has no merit either of simplicity or of subtlety in the choice of words; the main thought, the protection afforded by the dead bishop's bones, is set forth in the most unattractive fashion. And you must remember that the whole poem extends to twenty-one stanzas, of which I have only read you eight. Judged by any canons that we apply to religious literature, it is poor stuff. We must therefore remind ourselves once more of the great and lasting reputation of the author. This sort of thing was evidently what the Church wanted in the fourth century; and if it shows a lamentable standard of public taste, that is only our affair to the extent that we allow ourselves to be influenced by the judgments of that age in other departments of thought.

On one little matter we ought to do S. Ephraim justice. His humility is quite genuine. We have seen his belief in the value of relics. But he adjures his disciples in the curious piece known as his *Testament* or *Will* that they should not bury him in a Church under the altar, or among the ancient Martyrs and Confessors, but that he should be laid, wrapped in his old cloak, in the common cemetery among the strangers.

This is not the place to enter upon a general discussion of the works of S. Ephraim or to examine the genuineness of the enormous mass of material which has at various times been published under his name. But a word of warning on one point may not be out of place. I have already mentioned in the previous Lecture that a good deal of what has been printed as Ephraim's is not his, and you have seen from the specimen that I have just given that his genuine style does not readily lend itself to precise statements, suitable for illustrating his dogmatic position. It is always therefore most necessary when opinions or phrases are quoted as S. Ephraim's, or as illustrating the dogmatic beliefs of his age and country, to see whether they have been taken from works of undoubted genuineness. As an example of what I mean, I

GENUINE WORKS OF S. EPHRAIM

may mention that of five quotations intended to illustrate S. Ephraim's doctrine of the Eucharist, extracted by the late Dr Moberly from Dr Pusey's well-known collection, not one is taken from any of Ephraim's certainly authenticated writings, and I doubt if all of them are, as a matter of fact, really from his pen,[1] though very likely similar sentiments might be culled from his genuine works.

Let us therefore content ourselves with the certainly genuine works of this voluminous writer. You have probably had already enough of his poetry, and in what follows I shall chiefly confine myself to his prose. It is a curious fact that S. Ephraim is much more readable in his prose than in his verse. We are not continually fatigued with a series of those strained conceits which seem to have been as much admired by his contemporaries as the quaintnesses of Donne and Quarles were admired by the literary world of the time of James I.

The genuine theology of S. Ephraim is best studied from the work called *Sermo de Domino nostro*, edited by Lamy.[2] This is, in fact, a treatise on the Incarnation, and extracts from

---

[1] See *Journal of Theol. Studies* ii, p. 341.
[2] *Lamy* i 145-274; see also the Preface to Vol. ii. The Homily is translated by A. E. Johnston in Gwynn, pp. 305-330.

it are quoted by later writers such as Philoxenus, as from an acknowledged theological authority. To the Syrians it was known by the opening words: "Grace hath drawn near to blaspheming mouths and hath made them praise-giving harps. Wherefore let all mouths give praise to Him that withheld from them blasphemous discourse. To Thee be praise, that didst depart from one abode and dwell in another, to come and make us an abode for Him that sent Thee! The Only-begotten departed from the Divine Essence and dwelt in the Virgin, that by common birth the Only-begotten might become the Brother of many. And it was He that departed from Sheol and dwelt in the kingdom, that He might search out a way from Sheol the all-oppressing to that kingdom which is all-recompensing. For our Lord gave His resurrection as a pledge to mortal men, that He would remove them from Sheol that receives the dead without distinction to the kingdom that admits them that are invited with distinction, that from the place which treats alike the bodies of all men within it they may go to that which distinguishes the works of men within it." And again, he goes on to say: "He, the First-born, that had been born according to His own [Divine] Nature was born with another, a [human] birth beyond that which was natural to Him, that we in our turn might know that after our natural birth there is required for us another birth beyond what is natural to us. For He, as a spiritual being, until He came to material birth could not become material; and so also material beings, except they be born with another birth, cannot become spiritual." "Our Lord Himself," says Ephraim, "was born from the Godhead according to His own Nature; He was born from man contrary to His own Nature [that is, by miracle]; and He was born from Baptism extra-ordinarily; and the reason of this was that we might be born from man according to our nature, and from the Godhead contrary to our nature, and from the Spirit extra-ordinarily." "To Thee be praise," he says again, "who didst make of Thy Cross a bridge over Death, that souls might pass over it from the House of Death to the House of Life."

In these extracts you have, I think, most of the main ideas which underlie S. Ephraim's treatise. According to S. Ephraim, the object of the Incarnation, the taking of the Manhood into God, was that Christians might incorporate the Divine into their Manhood. We may notice that in Ephraim's view the doctrine of Christ's Nature and the doctrine of the Sacraments are inextricably intertwined. Jesus Christ receives the Spirit in baptism that we may also be born of the Spirit. He is the "Drug of Life" which Death swallowed[1] and could not retain—in other words, the φάρμακον ἀθανασίας of which Ignatius speaks (*ad Eph.* xx); thereby the gates of Sheol were opened, and the patriarchs of the Old Covenant were liberated. Yet Ephraim also applies the phrase metaphorically: "Our Lord," he says, "did not mingle with the eaters and drinkers for pleasure, as the Pharisees supposed, but that with the very food of mortal men He might mix His teaching as a Drug of Life."

It is really very difficult to extract from S. Ephraim any clear exposition of his views. He goes on from symbol to symbol, and the points he emphasises are sometimes striking, sometimes preposterous, but always fanciful. "Our Lord," he says,[2] "spat on His fingers and laid them in the ears of the deaf man and formed clay from His spittle and smeared it on the eyes of the blind man, that we might learn that by the leaven from the Body of Him who perfects all things hath what is lacking in our frame been

---

[1] *Lamy* i 155; the same idea is elaborated by Aphraates (*Hom.* xxii = *Wright*, p. 422).

[2] *Lamy* i 171; cf. Mk. vii 33 (in the Diatessaron) and Joh. ix 9.

supplied. It would not have been right for our Lord to cut off anything from His Body to fill up the imperfections of other bodies; but it was with what might be taken without loss from Him that He filled up the imperfections of the imperfect, even as with what can be eaten mortal men eat Him. Thus He filled up what was lacking and made alive what was dead, that we might know that from the Body in which true Fulness dwelt hath the imperfections of the imperfect been filled up, and from that same Body in which dwelt true Vitality hath life been given to mortal men." Thus the Eucharistic doctrine taught by Ephraim is that to come into real contact with and to absorb the Lord brings true life and true health to the Christian, just as physical contact with Him brought speech to the deaf and sight to the blind. The characteristic looseness of Ephraim's diction makes it always possible to hold that after all the words might be meant of spiritual feeding and absorbing, but the nature of the comparison of the Eucharistic bread with physical spittle makes it only too likely that Ephraim had chiefly in view the mere eating of the consecrated elements.

Another feature of S. Ephraim's Christology is his curious doctrine of what we may call the

Charismata, the spiritual privileges which had been as it were lent to Israel and were one by one resumed on earth by the Christ, their true Possessor. The early Christian theologians were fully convinced of the validity of Israel's hierarchy. The Jewish king was the Lord's Anointed, the Jewish priest was God's legitimate Minister, the Jewish prophet was the mouthpiece of the Holy Spirit. How then did our Lord give the priestly power to the disciples? From whom had He received the keys of the kingdom of Heaven which He gave to S. Peter.[1] It is curious to find S. Ephraim wondering, if only for a moment, whether Orders conferred by Christ were valid. The answer is equally strange. S. Ephraim tells us that the gift of Priesthood was given to our Lord in the Temple when Simeon took Him in his arms, or rather that the Lord then received back His own from Simeon, who having resigned the gift which had been committed to him was ready to depart in peace. "Thus," he continues, "each of the gifts that had been kept for the Son did He gather from their true tree. For He took away Baptism from the Jordan, though John afterwards still was baptizing; and He took the Priesthood from the Temple, though Hannan the High Priest still officiated therein; and He

---

[1] The question is actually asked in *Lamy* i 267.

took Prophecy that was being handed down among the just, though Caiaphas for a moment wove by means of it a crown for our Lord; and He took the kingdom from the house of David, even though Herod had been made his vicegerent. He it was, even our Lord, who flew down from on high; and when all these Gifts that He had given to them of old time saw Him, they flew and came from every side and alighted on Him their Giver, gathering themselves together from every side to come and engraft themselves on their true parent stem. . . . But when our Lord had taken His Priesthood from Israel, He hallowed with it all nations; and when He took away His Prophecy, He revealed by it His promises to all peoples; and when He bound on His Crown He fettered the strong man who took all captive and divided his spoils. These Gifts were useless to the Barren Fig-tree, so barren of fruit as to make barren even endowments like these: wherefore it was cut down without fruit, that these Gifts might go away and bring forth much fruit in all nations."

"Moreover," says Ephraim in conclusion, "from all local abodes hath He passed away, Who came to make our bodies into abodes for Him to dwell in. Let us therefore each one of us become dwelling-places, for, saith He, *whoso loveth Me, unto him will We come and an abode with him will We make.* This is the Godhead, for which, though all created things do not contain it, yet a lowly and humble mind doth suffice."[1]

The touch of piety and mysticism in this informal peroration should incline us, I think, to judge leniently of S. Ephraim's feeble philosophy and fanciful argumentation. But the philosophy is indeed very feeble, and the argumentation excessively fanciful. Aphraates sometimes makes us wish that the Church had been content to retain the simpler theology of earlier times; S. Ephraim shows us that the official expression of the belief of the Church needed co-ordination and precision. Without the Creeds I cannot help fearing that the theology of Ephraim might have led the Syriac-speaking Church into Tritheism. "Man," says he,[2] "is not left defenceless. The *Father* clothes him with armour, the *Son* makes him grasp the shield, the *Spirit* helps him in the contest." Sentences such as this may not be heretical; but they are worse. They are rhetorical, and rhetoric in theology leads direct to superstition. The theory of God's Nature as expressed by men in

---
[1] The MS. has *'aḥdân* (not *'aḳdân*) for "contain."
[2] *Ed. Rom.* v 319 C.

THE FANCIFULNESS OF S. EPHRAIM

human language must be at the best an imperfect presentiment, and the only value of the doctrines of the Trinity and of Christ's Divine and Human Personality is to help us less inadequately to realise the relations between ourselves and the mysterious Power outside us that rules the world, a Power which nevertheless we have been taught through Jesus Christ to call our Father. Doctrines such as these are things to be reverenced, or to be resolutely rejected; but for those who receive them they are not to be played with. They occupy a department of thought where "pretty fancies" are out of place, and S. Ephraim is full of pretty fancies. At the beginning of each of the six volumes of the Roman edition of his works is a charming copperplate in the style of the eighteenth century, showing the Saint seated under a spreading tree, with little winged *amoretti* hastening down with scrolls of inspiration direct from Heaven. The saint receives them with humility, while a couple of his disciples in the background look on in astonishment at the miracle. It is all very nice, and its only fault is that it is totally unlike the facts of the case. So it is with Ephraim's theology. It is out of touch with reality; it gives us neither the historical Christ, nor the Christianity of the early Church, nor yet the clearly defined doctrines of post-Nicene times. In a word, S. Ephraim represents the transitional age to which he belonged. His fatal want of intellectual seriousness helps to explain to us why his Church became strongly orthodox under Rabbûla, and yet sank permanently a hundred years later into heterodoxy and schism.

The intellectual atmosphere of Rabbûla is indeed very different from that of S. Ephraim. Both men were ascetics, but there the resemblance comes to an end. Rabbûla is the very incarnation of clear-cut and regulated ecclesiasticism. I do not know that I can illustrate his position better than by the sermon he is said to have preached at Constantinople in the open church while Nestorius was still Patriarch.[1] "Two are the chief commandments, my beloved brethren," he says "those in which the law and the prophets are exhausted. The first is that thou shalt love the Lord thy God from all thy heart. He therefore that loveth doth not investigate but obeys, and he doth not scrutinise but believes. For not by words is God loved

---

[1] *Overbeck*, p. 198, l. 21 ff. The quotation is taken from *Overbeck*, p. 241 f. The sermon itself seems to have been delivered in Syriac (p. 241, l. 12).

but by deeds, for (saith He) *He that loveth Me keepeth My commandments*. The other of the two that is like to it is that thou shalt love thy neighbour as thyself. He that loveth doth not kill, doth not steal, doth not commit adultery, neither doth he lie or covet, for that which he doth not wish to be done to him by anyone he himself doth not to others, but as he would that men should do to him, he also so doth to them seeing that he loveth them. These things are the profitable doctrines for our souls, my brethren, and are what is useful for the building of the whole Church of the Messiah. Wherefore unto them must we direct our attention at all times in our works, for these alone form the good store of our true righteousness." All this is quite in the style of Aphraates himself. "But," continues Rabbûla, "because I know your ears and your attention are expecting to hear our word and our faith, and are desirous to know our truth in the Messiah, we are compelled out of love for you to speak before you the things which in the silence only of faith should be honoured. The inquiry, therefore, of your request is this: 'Whether the Virgin Mary be the Mother of God in truth, or is called so in name only, or whether she ought not to be so named?' Now we," said Rabbûla, "in what we are sure of have hoped, for it is our life, and with confidence we have believed, for it is indeed our boast; and we say with uplifted voice without deception, that Mary IS the Mother of God, and with justice her name should be so heralded, for she became on earth Mother to God the Word by His Will,[1] even to Him who according to the course of nature had no Mother in heaven. For *God sent His Son and He was born of a woman* crieth the Apostle. Now if anyone dare to say that according to the course of nature she gave birth to God the Word, not only doth he not say well, but wrongly doth he make confession. For 'Mother of God' we call the holy Virgin, not because according to the course of nature she gave birth to the Godhead, but because God the Word was born from her when He became a man. *For lo*, it saith, *the Virgin shall conceive and shall bear a son, and His name shall be called Immanuel, which is interpreted* 'Our God with us.' But this does not mean that from the blessed Virgin our Lord obtained His first beginning, for the Word was in the beginning with the Father, as John testifies; but that from her appeared the Messiah in the flesh through His loving-kindness, who Himself is God over all according to the course of nature."

---

[1] Read *leh* not *lâh* in *Overbeck*, p. 242, line 16.

This long extract I have given in full, not to criticise its theology from a modern standpoint, but to compare its tone with what I have previously read from Aphraates and from Ephraim. I think you will all be sensible of the difference. What we have heard from Aphraates and from Ephraim is the natural utterance of the East: what we have heard from Rabbûla is the voice of Greek philosophy, arguing, from *data* furnished by texts taken from Canonical writings, about Substance and Nature and other figments of the philosophical mind.

To criticise adequately such an utterance as this of Rabbûla's would need not only more philosophical knowledge but also more sympathy with the course of fifth century controversy than I possess. There can, I venture to think, be little doubt that it is genuine, for it accurately represents the ecclesiastical position of the great Bishop of Edessa. That he should ultimately take the anti-Nestorian side is not surprising when we read S. Ephraim's Hymns on the Nativity. But Rabbûla may very well have been sincere, when he deprecated discussion upon the precise degree of honour which was to be paid to the Virgin. For Rabbûla she was truly *Theotokos*, but he would have preferred not to discuss the question, as the people of Constantinople were accustomed to discuss such questions, in the Hippodrome or in the Theatre, as interesting points for disputation. Rabbûla's mind was severely practical. He disapproved of the Theatre and the Circus, and "the disgusting spectacle of wild beasts shedding human blood in the Stadium he altogether suppressed by his authoritative command" (Life, *Overbeck*, 179). To such a one the atmosphere of Constantinople must have been profoundly distasteful, and no doubt his visit confirmed him in his opposition to the then popular religion of the capital.

What Rabbûla loved above all other things was Order. The force of popular sentiment induced him to choose the anti-Nestorian side, but in either case he would have taken care to regularise the ordinances of his diocese. Practically this meant the assimilation of what he found in Edessa to what was done in Antioch and the other great centres of the Greek-speaking Church. So far as in him lay Edessa, and with it the rest of Syriac-speaking Christianity, ceased to be cut off by its Bible, its Liturgy, its Doctrine, its party Watchwords, from the other Churches of the Empire.

But for this his Church paid a heavy penalty. It ceased to have any independent life or thought. From the fifth century onwards Syriac-speaking Christianity is wholly derivative and secondary. The Greek theology does not sit well on the Syriac mind, nor does it sound well in the Syriac language. Nor again, as I have already remarked, were the Syrians able to keep step with Constantinople. Judged by the standard of Chalcedonian Orthodoxy they all fell into error. Fifty years after Rabbûla's death in 435 you would hardly have been able to find a Syriac-speaking Christian community which was in full communion with the Byzantine Church. Those who lived within the Persian dominions were almost all Nestorians; those who lived within the Roman Empire were almost all Monophysites. The edifice which Rabbûla had reared was ruined in the hands of his successors, and the external unity of the Christian Church of the East came to pieces, never again to be welded together.

In the next Lecture we shall consider the view of the Christian Life and Sacraments which prevailed in the early Syriac-speaking Church, a part of our subject where far more individuality was shown by the Syrians than in the Christological disputes. To-day I would end by quoting to you the peroration of S. Ephraim's

Commentary on the Book of Genesis, a passage eminently characteristic of his thought and style. It is orthodox, and yet it retains in its doxology the earlier form of invocation; it is fanciful and out of touch with the view of the older Hebrew literature with which modern criticism has made us familiar, and yet in its expression of a general purpose animating ancient history it forms a not undignified conclusion to a detailed exposition. "Now to God," says Ephraim (*Ed. Rom.* iv 115), "Who through His Son created all creatures out of nothing, and wrote not this Book of Genesis at the beginning, because these things had come within the cognisance of Adam, and each generation delivered them to that which came after, as it had learnt from that which had gone before; but seeing that all had strayed from God and God's creative work had been forgotten by all, He wrote these things through Moses for the people of the Hebrews after they had changed Nature, that He might bear witness to the creation of Nature —to Him, I say, that wrote in the desert the things that had been manifested in the mind of Adam while yet in Paradise, from the ancient peoples that without book had known these things, and from the intermediate people of the Hebrews that through the book heard and believed them, and from us the latter peoples that have entered into the possession of their book, yea, from those that yet have remained in the rebellion of their heathen sacrifices, to Him and to His Messiah and to His Holy Spirit be glory and honour now and at all times and for ever and ever, Amen and Amen."

LECTURE IV

MARRIAGE AND THE SACRAMENTS

THE very earliest Christianity was not ascetic. John the Baptist had come in the way of righteousness, but our Lord's way of life was in the eyes of His contemporaries lax. He lived among men and with men, and the call to renunciation which He made upon His more immediate followers was brought out rather by the course of events than by the normal fitness of things. Sympathy with the poor and abstinence from selfish anxiety was always the teaching of Jesus Christ, but the wickedness of enjoyment in itself was not part of His Gospel; His Beatitude is "Blessed are the hungry," not "Blessed are the fasting."

The opposition between the Galilean Prophet and the leaders of the Jewish world, both political and religious, grew rapidly more acute, and it was with the certainty of temporal failure that our Lord went up to His last Passover at Jerusalem. He was profoundly unwilling that

CHRIST AND ASCETICISM

any one of His followers should accompany Him without counting the cost. It was to no earthly triumph that He was leading them, and so He tells them again and again on the journey that those who come with Him must be prepared to lose everything. Yet even on this journey His first reply to the rich young man who asked what he ought to do, was simply that he should keep the Ten Commandments; in other words, our Lord's general counsels remained what they had always been. He was willing further to accept the young man as a personal follower if he felt himself equal to the strain, but wealth and respectability were at that crisis useless encumbrances.

It is quite in accordance with all this that we find Jesus asserting at this very same time the inviolability of marriage, and that among all the many possessions which the disciples are praised for having cheerfully forsaken—house, brethren, sisters, mother, father, children, lands,—the *wife* is conspicuously absent.[1] Grant that the Wife is practically implied in the House, the fact remains that according to the earliest Gospel and the best authority our Lord deliberately refrained from praising a man for forsaking his wife, even to follow Him.

---

[1] Both in Mark x 29 and Matt. xix 29 the evidence for the omission of ἢ γυναῖκα is overwhelming.

A very different tendency soon showed itself in parts at least of the Christian community. The married state was thought of as being incompatible with the highest life, and this view actually shows itself in the form of words ascribed to Christ. This is quite markedly the case in the Gospel according to S. Luke. In this Gospel the words "or wife" is supplied after "house,"[1] and the reply of Jesus to the Sadducees is so worded as to make it appear that those that are worthy to attain the resurrection from the dead do not marry like the ordinary inhabitants of this world. According to S. Mark our Lord says "when they shall rise from the dead they neither marry nor are given in marriage," but in S. Luke the words of the answer are: "The sons of this world marry and are given in marriage; but they that are accounted worthy to attain to that world and the resurrection from the dead neither marry nor are given in marriage."[2]

It is a far cry from S. Luke to Aphraates, a gap of some two hundred and forty years. But after all the writings of Aphraates form the earliest Syriac authority of any considerable extent, of

---

[1] Luke xviii 29.
[2] Luke xx 34, 35; cf. Luke xvi 8. In this Gospel the Resurrection is only a "resurrection of the just" (Luke xiv 14).

which we know the date and can trust the authenticity. It will be convenient, therefore, to begin with Aphraates once more, and work backwards and forwards from him.

The Church of which Aphraates was a leader offered many features which to us are quite familiar. It had Bishops, Priests and Deacons. Much of the teaching which we find in Aphraates about the Sacraments is just what might have been expected from a leading ecclesiastic of the fourth century. But this cannot be said of everything that we find in his writings. As in the case of his doctrine of the Trinity and of the person of Christ, it is not so much the orthodoxy or the heterodoxy as the independence of Aphraates which strikes the modern reader. The good bishop goes on in his easy simple style with a tone of assured authority and unconsciousness of serious opposition, and it is only when we pause and try to fit his utterances into the schemes of doctrine and practice with which we are familiar that we realise that we are moving in another world. The Church of Aphraates, like the Church of S. Athanasius, is the legitimate child of second century Christianity, but it has come by another line of descent, and the cousins have not all things in common.

With regard to the Lord's Supper Aphraates

tells us that in the Eucharist the faithful partake of the Body and Blood of the Christ. It must be taken fasting, and the fast must be such as was once for all prescribed by Isaiah, "for always is fasting from evil things better than fasting from bread and water."[1] The fasting of Abel and Enoch, of innocent Noah, of faithful Abraham, of unrevengeful Joseph are to be our models. "If purity of heart be absent, the fast is not accepted. And remember and see, my beloved, that it is well that a man should cleanse his heart and keep his tongue and cleanse his hands of evil; for it is not fitting to mix honey and wormwood. For if a man would fast from bread and water, let him not mix with his fasting abuse and curses. Thou hast but one door to thy house, that house which is a Temple of God; it doth not beseem thee, O man, that by the door where the King doth enter in should come forth filth and dirt! For when a man will fast from all that is abominable and will take the Body and Blood of the Messiah, let him take heed to his mouth whereby the King's Son doth enter in. Thou hast no right, O man, through that same mouth to give out unclean words! Hear what our Saviour saith: *That which entereth into a man doth not defile him;*

---
[1] III 8.

EUCHARISTIC DOCTRINE IN APHRAATES 123

but that which cometh forth from the mouth, that defileth him." [1] The fast here prescribed is metaphorical, but there can be no doubt that Aphraates teaches the doctrine that Jesus Christ is really present in the consecrated elements.

The view of the Eucharist taken by Aphraates may further be illustrated from his singular and fanciful explanation of the three days and three nights among the dead which our Lord had predicted for Himself. In the discourse on the Passover [2] he says that our Lord gave His Body and Blood to the disciples at the Last Supper. But, he argues, he whose body is eaten [3] and blood drunk must be already counted among the dead. The three days and three nights are to be reckoned from the time of the Supper, and, as Aphraates puts the three hours' darkness as one whole night and the ensuing time of light on Good Friday afternoon as one whole day, he has no difficulty in making up the required number. Thus Christ both celebrates the Jewish Passover with His disciples and is yet Himself the Paschal Lamb. Moreover, adds Aphraates, this is why He kept silence before Pilate and

---

[1] III 1.

[2] XII 6, 7.

[3] In XII 9 (*Wright*, p. 222, line 3) we must read 'aχîl: the MS. has 'eχal (or 'âχêl).

the Jews, for it was not fitting that one who is counted among the dead should speak. These things, however, belong to the curiosities of exegesis. Their chief bearing upon the history of Christian Doctrine is that this whole chain of fanciful reasoning assumes quite crudely the real presence of Christ in what He gave to the Twelve at the Supper.

But it is in the theory of Baptism as held by Aphraates that we come definitely in touch with the view of Christian life to which I referred at the beginning of this Lecture. The majority of the references to Baptism in Aphraates contain little that is startling. Christian baptism is the true circumcision;[1] it is administered in the Names of the Three Persons of the Trinity;[2] by baptism regeneration is conferred, sins are washed away,[3] and the body is preserved in the Day of Judgment.[4] "From baptism do we receive the Spirit of the Messiah. For in the same hour that the priests invoke the Spirit, the heavens open and it cometh down and broodeth upon the waters, and they that are baptized are clothed with it. For from all that are born of the body the

---

[1] XII 9.
[2] XXIII 63: see above, p. 87.
[3] IV 19.
[4] VI 14.

Spirit is far away, until they come to the Birth by water, and then they receive the Holy Spirit."[1] In accordance with ancient custom the rite of baptism is performed at Easter.[2]

All this is normal and regular, almost commonplace. It is when we go on to inquire who were the recipients of baptism that we find ourselves in another world. In Aphraates, Baptism is not the common seal of every Christian's faith, but a privilege reserved for celibates.

The passage where this amazing view is most clearly enforced is so important for our understanding of early oriental Christianity that I give it at length. In the Discourse on Penitents, after reciting the story of Gideon, who prefigured the mystery of Baptism when by the trial of water he picked out his three hundred from ten thousand men, and after quoting our Lord's words that many are called but few chosen, Aphraates goes on to say:[3] "Wherefore thus should the trumpeters, the heralds of the Church cry and warn all the Society of God before the Baptism—them, I say, that have offered themselves for virginity and for holiness, youths and maidens holy — them shall the heralds warn.

---
[1] VI 14: cf. *Gwynn*, p. 371.   [2] XII 13.
[3] VII 20 (*Wright*, p. 147 f.).

And they shall say: 'He whose heart is set to the state of matrimony, let him marry before baptism, lest he fall in the spiritual contest and be killed. And he that feareth this part of the struggle, let him turn back, lest he break his brother's heart like his own. He also that loveth his possessions let him turn back from the army, lest when the battle shall wax too fierce for him he remember his property and turn back, and he that turneth back then is covered with disgrace. He that hath not offered himself and hath not yet put on his armour, if he turn back he is not blamed; but every one that offereth himself and putteth on his armour, if he turn back from the contest becometh a laughing-stock.'"

This is a strange exhortation, strange at least to us Westerns. Perhaps it was not so much Constantine's fault as the fault of his spiritual advisers that his famous baptism was so long delayed. Those who are not yet baptized are not blamed by Aphraates; if they wish to marry, let them do so, but in that case they must not volunteer for the sacramental life.

The deliberate reservation of baptism for the spiritual aristocracy of Christendom shows us that we are dealing with a view of the sacraments quite other than the Catholic view. For it is not merely a question of the theoretical exaltation of the celibate above the married state, or an exhortation to a superior morality, as some critics of mine suggested when I first drew attention to the doctrinal importance of the passage in the little book called *Early Christianity outside the Roman Empire*.[1] The important thing is that people who intend to marry are warned off from receiving baptism and are actually recommended to go away and sow their wild oats, because the married life and the life of the baptized Christian are quite incompatible! The Christian community, therefore, according to Aphraates, consists of baptized celibates, together with a body of adherents who remain outside and are not really members of the body.

However clear the meaning of the passage from the Discourse on Penitents may be, I can hardly expect it to be estimated at its full weight without supporting this strange conception of the Church from other Syriac sources. To do this, it will first be necessary to come to a clear view of the meaning of a term which very often occurs in Syriac ecclesiastical literature.

---

[1] P. 51. Nearly the whole of the first part of this Lecture will be found there, and I have not seen any reason to change my views on the subject.

This term is *bar Q'yâmâ*, literally "Son of the Covenant" (or, "Son of a Covenant"), but generally rendered by "Monk." We shall not gain any accurate idea of the early Syriac Christian Church until we trace somewhat precisely what was at various times denoted by *bar Q'yâmâ*.

The Syriac language is quite rich in words for monks and nuns. For "coenobite," *i.e.* a monk who lives in a religious community, we have *dayrâyâ*, a word regularly formed from *dayrâ*, "monastery." For "eremite" or "solitary" we have *îḥîdâyâ*. For "anchorite" or "recluse" we have *ḥ'βîshâ* and *ḥ'βîshâyâ*. A "Stylite," like the famous Simeon, was called *esṭônâyâ* or *esṭônârâ*. And there are naturally the corresponding terms in the feminine, to denote the various kinds of nuns. With all this wealth of nomenclature it is antecedently probable that *bar Q'yâmâ*, and in the feminine *bath Q'yâmâ*, must not simply mean "monk" and "nun," but must have a more definite and specialised meaning.

The first answer that may be given, to diverge for a moment into a brief etymological discussion, is that *bar Q'yâmâ* is a Canon or Regular, *i.e.* a Christian who lives under a special Rule, such as the Rule of S. Basil or of S. Benedict. Thus we

THE SONS OF THE COVENANT

find in the Syriac translation of the 15th decree of the Synod of Laodicæa that *b'nai Q'yâmâ* (the plural of *bar Q'yâmâ*) corresponds to κανονικοί in the Greek. This is very good so far as it goes, but it does not answer the real question. For we shall have to go on and ask: Who were the Regulars of the early Syriac Church? Under what rule did they live?

The answer to these questions I believe to be very simple. I believe the *B'nai Q'yâmâ* were simply the baptized laity of the early Syriac-speaking Church, and that in the earlier stages of that Church's development no layman was accepted for baptism unless he was prepared to lead a life of strict continence and freedom from worldly cares. This meant that, except for the more or less exceptional case of young devotees who felt they had a "vocation," the average Christian looked forward to becoming a full Church member only at a somewhat advanced age, and as a prelude to retiring morally and physically from the life of this world.

At a later period the theory of the Christian life changed. When Christianity was no longer a proscribed sect but had become in one form or another the State religion, the mass of the adherents of the Church wished to make the best of both worlds. They were anxious to obtain the benefits of baptism all their lives. Parents also had their children baptized in infancy, for whom by reason of their age special vows were inappropriate. Thus a Christian community sprang into existence, of which by far the greater number, both of old and young, were actually baptized, though only a minority were specially addicted to religion in the modern sense of the term. The old-fashioned *B'nai Q'yâmâ* still continued, but they now became a sort of monastic order in the community, instead of the community itself. Living as they did among ordinary human beings, and not like the Hermits in the desert or the Cœnobites in a separate society, it became the duty of bishops like Rabbûla to devise rules for the regulation of their course of life.

I propose now to illustrate these statements from Syriac documents of various kinds. Let us begin with the *Doctrine of Addai*, a work which, as we saw in the first of these Lectures, cannot be used as an accurate narrative of historical events, but can at least be taken as giving an ideal picture of the early Christian community at Edessa. In the *Doctrine of Addai*, then, we read (p. 47) that "all the Society[1] of

---

[1] In Syriac *Q'yâmâ*. Dr Phillips translates the word "chiefs," but without authority.

men and of women were modest and decorous, and they were holy and pure and singly and modestly were they dwelling without spot, in the watchfulness of the ministry decorously, in their care for the poor, in their visitations for the sick." In the ideal picture drawn of the Church in the time of Addai the Apostle we hear nothing of any provision for young Christian children, nothing of the duties of Christian parents, no provision for Christian schools.

The next document we come to is the *Martyrdom of Shamôna and Guria*. We have seen that this document, which belongs to the year 297, is really the earliest historical narrative relating to the Syriac Church which has come down to us in approximately its original form. As such it is particularly interesting, and all the more so since the whole action takes place before the Edicts of Toleration and the accession of Constantine. In the very first sentence of this work we meet with the *B'nâth Q'yâmâ*, the "Daughters of the Covenant." We read that "in the days of Qônâ, Bishop of Edessa, the wicked Diocletian had made a great and strong persecution against all the Churches of the Messiah, so that the priests and deacons with bitter afflictions were tormented, and the *b'nâth Q'yâmâ* and the cloistered nuns[1] in bitter exposure were standing, and all the Christians were in affliction and grief."

The Martyrdom goes on to tell how Guria and Shamôna were arrested, and how valiantly they confessed and were martyred. Guria was from Sargi, and Shamôna from Gannada or Gagnada, both apparently names of villages near Edessa. Shamôna is merely introduced as the friend or companion of Guria, but Guria is further distinguished by the epithet *m'qadd'shâ* i.e. "hallowed." *Holy* is used again and again for *continent* in Syriac ecclesiastical literature. Before the martyrdom, therefore, Guria was regarded as in some way more holy than Shamôna, and what that way was we learn at the end of the story after their execution. There it is casually mentioned that Shamôna had a daughter. Thus the ascetic sentiment is indicated most clearly: Guria, the celibate, is "holy," Shamôna, who has a daughter, is not.

We now come to Aphraates himself. He has a whole Discourse (No. VI) on the *B'nai Q'yâmâ*, and the position it occupies in the series of Discourses is significant. First come the

---

[1] Syriac *Dayrâyâthâ*: these do not appear in the Armenian version of the Martyrdom and perhaps should be omitted.

Discourses on the primary duties of Faith, Love, Fasting, and Prayer. Then a Discourse on the burning question of the great war between Rome and Persia then raging, a war which seemed as if it were actually ushering in the last times. Then come two Discourses on the Christian Community, followed up by three short Discourses on the Resurrection, on Humility, and a final address "to Pastors,'' which is really a kind of peroration to the First Book of Aphraates. The Christian Community is divided by Aphraates for practical purposes into two parts, the *B'nai Q'yâmâ* and the Penitents. And as far as I can see, these correspond to the Baptized and the Catechumens.

Aphraates begins without preamble by a general exhortation to the Christian life addressed to those who have "taken up the yoke of the Saints." He reminds them that the Adversary is skilful, but he says:[1] "All the children of Light are without fear of him, because the darkness flies from before the light. The children of the Good fear not the Evil One, for He hath given him to be trampled by their feet. When he makes himself like darkness unto them they become light; and

---

[1] *Wright*, p. 108; *Gwynn*, p. 365, where the whole Discourse is translated.

when he creeps upon them like a serpent, they become salt, whereof he cannot eat.[1] . . . If he comes in upon them in the lust of food, they conquer him by fasting like our Saviour. And if he wishes to contend with them by the lust of the eyes, they lift up their eyes to the height of heaven. . . . If he wishes to come against them by sleep, they are wakeful and vigilant and sing psalms and pray. If he allures them by possessions, they give them to the poor. If he comes in as sweetness against them, they taste it not, knowing that he is bitter. If he inflames them with the desire of Eve, they dwell alone and not with the daughters of Eve."[2]

Then follows a list of the mischief that the Bible tells us has been done by Eve and her daughters. Aphraates reminds us in a passage which I quote because it is so characteristic of his style that "it was through Eve that Satan came in upon Adam, and Adam was enticed because of his inexperience. And again he came in against Joseph through his master's wife, but Joseph was acquainted with his craftiness and would not afford him a hearing. Through a woman he fought with Samson until he took away his Naziriteship. Reuben was

---

[1] This fanciful comparison occurs several times in Aphraates.
[2] P. 365.

the first-born of all his brethren, and through
his father's wife the adversary cast a blemish
upon him. Aaron was the great high-priest of
the House of Israel, and through Miriam his
sister he envied Moses. Moses was sent to
deliver the people from Egypt, and he took
with him the woman who advised him to
shameful acts, and the Lord met with Moses
and desired to slay him, till he sent back his
wife to Midian. David was victorious in all
his battles, yet by means of a daughter of Eve
there was found a blemish in him. Amnon was
beautiful and fair in countenance, yet the
adversary took him captive by desire for his
sister, and Absalom slew him on account of
the humbling of Tamar. Solomon was greater
than all the kings of the earth, yet in the
days of his old age his wives led him astray.
Through Jezebel, daughter of Ethbaal, the
wickedness of Ahab was increased and he
became exceedingly polluted. Furthermore the
adversary tempted Job through his children
and his possessions, and when he could not
prevail over him he went and brought against
him his panoply, and he came bringing with
him a daughter of Eve who had caused Adam
to sink, and through her mouth he said to
Job, her righteous husband, *Curse God.* But

Job rejected her counsel. King Asa also conquered the Accursed-of-life, when he wished to come in against him through his mother. For Asa knew his craftiness and removed his mother from her high estate and cut in pieces her idol and cast it down. John was greater than all the prophets, yet Herod slew him because of the dancing of a daughter of Eve. Haman was wealthy and third in honour from the king, yet his wife counselled him to destroy the Jews. Zimri was head of the tribe of Simeon, yet Cozbi, daughter of the chiefs of Midian, overthrew him, and because of one woman twenty-four thousand of Israel fell in one day."

After this lengthy catalogue Aphraates goes on to say:[1] "Therefore my brethren, every man that is a *bar Q'yâmâ* or a saint that loves the solitary life, and at the same time wishes that a woman that is a *bath Q'yâmâ* like himself should dwell with him, in that case it were better for him to take a wife openly and not wanton in lust; and a woman also in that case it behoves her, if she depart not from a man who is a solitary, that openly she be taken to wife. Woman with woman ought to dwell, and man with man should dwell. And the man too that wishes to be in holiness, let not his wife dwell with him, lest he

---
[1] *Gwynn*, p. 366; *Wright*, p. 111.

turn back to his former nature and be accounted an adulterer. Wherefore this counsel is proper and right and fair which I counsel unto myself and also to you, my beloved, solitaries that take no wives and virgins that are not taken to wife and they that love holiness; it is just and right and proper that even if a man be in distress he should be by himself, and so it becometh him to dwell as is written in Jeremiah the prophet: *Blessed is the man that shall bear Thy yoke in his youth, and shall sit by himself and keep silence because he hath received Thy yoke.*[1] For so, my beloved, it becometh him that beareth the yoke of the Messiah that he should keep His yoke in purity."

It is scarcely necessary to add that in this "taking to wife" and "being taken to wife" no religious service is implied. There was no sacrament of Holy Matrimony in Aphraates' religious system. In the *Introduction* to Dom Parisot's edition of Aphraates the learned Benedictine finds traces of all the Catholic sacraments except this one. The omission is not accidental. I venture to think Aphraates would have considered a marriage service as irrational and unseemly as a Sacrament of Usury or of Military Service. He only recognises two

[1] Lam. iii 27, 28.

grades in the Christian ranks, the baptized celibate (from whose ranks also the clergy are drawn) and the unbaptized penitent. "By the coming of the offspring of the Blessed Mary," he goes on to say,[1] "the thorns are uprooted and the sweat taken away, and the fig-tree cursed and the dust made salt, and the curse is nailed to the Cross, and the edge of the sword taken away from before the Tree of Life and food given to the faithful and Paradise promised to the blessed and to virgins and saints, and the fruits of the Tree of Life are given as food to the faithful and to the virgins and to those that do the will of God. . . . For those that do not take wives are ministered by the Watchers of Heaven; those that keep holiness rest in the sanctuary of the Most High; all the solitaries doth the Only One from the bosom of His Father make to rejoice. There is there neither male nor female, neither bond nor free, but all of them are sons of the Most High. And all the pure virgins that have been betrothed to the Messiah, there they light their torches and with the Bridegroom do they enter the marriage chamber. . . . The wedding-feast of the daughters of Eve is for seven days, but theirs is the Bridegroom that doth not withdraw for

---

[1] *Gwynn*, p. 367; *Wright*, p. 113 ff.

ever. The adornment of the daughters of Eve is wool that wears out and perishes, but theirs is clothing that doth not wear out. The beauty of the daughters of Eve, old age doth wither it, but their beauty in the time of the resurrection is renewed."

"O virgins who have betrothed yourselves to the Messiah," continues Aphraates, "when one of the *b'nai Q'yâmâ* shall say to one of you 'I will dwell with thee, and thou minister to me,' thus shalt thou say to him: 'To a royal Husband am I betrothed, and to Him do I minister; and if I leave his ministry and minister to thee, my Betrothed will be wroth with me and will write me a letter of divorce and will dismiss me from His house, and while thou seekest to be honoured by me and I to be honoured by thee, see lest hurt come upon me and thee. *Take not fire in thy bosom lest it burn thy garments*, but be thou in honour by thyself and I will be by myself in honour.'"

There are many other general directions given by Aphraates in the rest of his Discourse for the conduct of the *B'nai Q'yâmâ*, but they do not call for special remark here. The rule of life which he sketches out is quiet, dignified, and temperate, with no special features of observance or asceticism. But I have quoted largely from the parts which deal with his view of the relations, or rather the absence of relations, between man and woman, because they are of the essence of his view of the Christian life, and because nothing but a rather full method of quotation would sufficiently illustrate his attitude. And here I must once again emphasise the importance of the passage in the Seventh Discourse with which I set out, where Aphraates dissuades those who intend to marry from coming to baptism.[1] That is the decisive point which separates these exhortations from later works such as the Discourses of Philoxenus or S. Benedict's rule itself. "Priests and scribes and sages, call and say to all the people: let him that hath betrothed a wife and doth wish to take her, let him turn back and rejoice with his wife,"[2] says Aphraates, and the call is a call to Baptism. The Christian community with all its privileges and blessings is on this theory restricted to celibates who have as much as possible withdrawn from the world: the mass of the people stand outside. Not only Art, Science, and Politics, but also the Hearth and the Home, are shut out from the province of Religion.

---

[1] See above, p. 126.
[2] *Wright*, p. 146. The words are a paraphrase of Deut. xx 7.

Before we criticise this view of life let us remember that it is well known outside the Catholic Church. The Buddhist Community is essentially a Community of monks, who alone constitute the congregation of the faithful. The people stand by the side and honour the saints, but they themselves do not tread the Path. And to come to what is really nearer home, the same state of things that is contemplated by Aphraates actually obtained among the Marcionites during the three hundred years and more of their existence as an organised body. It had always been a puzzle to me how the Marcionites maintained their numbers, for their way of life must have been strict or their Catholic opponents would have accused them of vice. Doubtless the greater number of them entered religion late in life, forsaking their families as Rabbûla did. As with Aphraates, the followers of Marcion admitted to baptism only those who intended for the remainder of their days to lead a celibate life.[1] Marriage to the Marcionites meant spiritual marriage to Christ: the connexions formed before baptism among Marcionite

---

[1] Cf. Tertullian *adv. Marcionem* iv 34 (on Luke xvi 18): "Aut si omnino negas permitti diuortium a Christo, quomodo tu nuptias dirimis, nec coniungens marem et feminam nec alibi coniunctos ad sacramentum baptismatis et eucharistiae admittens nisi inter se coniurauerint aduersus fructum nuptiarum?"

adherents were not recognised by the Marcionite Church, which consisted only of the Baptized. It is worth notice that among the many faults found by S. Ephraim in his polemic against Marcion and his followers their rejection of Christian marriage is not included.

The same system also prevailed among the Manichees, who were divided into the "Elect" and the "Hearers." The "Elect" were alone fully initiated, and they also were ascetics, celibate, and living on herbs provided for them by the inferior class of "Hearers." Their reputed descendants, the Albigenses in the South of France, still continued the separation between the ascetic Elect and the ordinary disciples, and the rite of admission to the order of the Elect was called by them spiritual Christian baptism.[1]

To return to the Syriac-speaking Church and the history of the *B'nai Q'yâmâ*. Aphraates is the last witness to the old order of things. After his time, and perhaps before his time within the Syriac-speaking provinces of the Roman Empire, married persons were admitted to baptism, and conversely baptism and the reception of the Lord's Supper was no longer regarded as a

---

[1] See the Ritual of *Consolamentum*, as given in F. C. Conybeare's *Key of Truth*, Appendix vi, pp. 160-170.

bar to matrimony. At what date the Church in the East actually came to bless the ceremony of betrothal I have not been able to discover. What is more easy to trace is the gradual decay of the *b'nai Q'yâmâ*, as shown by the rules which Rabbûla found it necessary to draw up for them.

These rules are found in a work called *Commands and Admonitions to Priests and to Sons of the Covenant living in the country*,[1] and no better way could be found of getting an accurate picture of the Mesopotamian Church early in the fifth century than by the study of them, both by what Rabbûla commands and by what he thinks it necessary to forbid.

1. "First of all," says Rabbûla, "let the Sons of the Church know the True Faith of Holy Church, that they be not led astray by heretics.

2. "Let not any of the Periodeutæ or the Priests and Deacons or of the Sons of the Covenant dwell with women, save with his mother or his sister or with his daughter, and let them not make households for these women outside their own establishment and let them persevere in living with these women."

Apparently therefore the ecclesiastic was not to live with a married sister, or to live with one sister after another.

3. "Let not Priests and Deacons and Sons of the Covenant

---
[1] *Overbeck*, pp. 215-221.

compel the Daughters of the Covenant to weave garments for them against their will.

4. "Let not Priests and Deacons be ministered to by women, and specially by the Daughters of the Covenant.

5. "Let not Priests and Deacons and Periodeutæ take a bribe from anyone, and specially from those who are bringing a suit [before them]."

The Periodeutes was a sort of Visitor, something between a Suffragan Bishop and a Rural Dean.

6. "Let not Priests and Deacons make collections either from the Sons of the Covenant or from laymen, even if commanded by those of the city, but let the needs of the Church be filled by him who gives of his own free will.

7. "When the Bishop comes to a village, let them not make collections from laymen in the Bishop's name; but if there be anything in the Church let them pay what suffices from the Church's funds, and if there be nothing in the Church let them not give anything.

9. "Let not Priests and Deacons and Sons of the Covenant and Daughters of the Covenant demand interest or usury or any trades of filthy lucre.

10. "Let not the Sons of the Covenant or the Daughters of the Covenant allow their Priests to dwell with laymen save with their relatives only, or with one another.

11. "Let all the Sons of the Church persevere in fasting and be instant in prayer: let them have care for the poor and require justice for the oppressed without respect of persons.

12. "Let all the Priests in the villages have care for the poor that betake themselves to them, and especially those that are Sons of the Covenant.

16. "In every Church there is, let a house be known in

which the poor that betake themselves thither can rest; but diviners and wizards and those who write charms and anoint men and women under the pretence of making cures drive out from every place, and exact from them promises that they will not invade our dominions.

17. "Let not the Daughters of the Covenant be allowed to come or go to Church alone by night, but if possible let them dwell with one another; and so also with the Sons of the Covenant.

18. "If there be any of the Sons of the Covenant or of the Daughters of the Covenant in need, let the Priests or Deacons of their villages take care of them; but if he is not able to do so, let him inform us that we may provide for them, lest because of their need they may be compelled to do something that is not suitable."

It is evident from this that it was the exception for a Son or Daughter of the Covenant to be in actual want: evidently they took no express vow of poverty.

19. "Let the Sons of the Covenant learn the Psalms and the Daughters of the Covenant learn Hymns also.

20. "Let not Priests or Deacons or Sons of the Covenant and Daughters of the Covenant pronounce the Name of God[1] and swear, neither in falsehood nor in truth, but (let their speech be) as is commanded."

The reference, of course, is to the Sermon on the Mount, but the phrase about not pronouncing the Name of God is curiously Jewish in tone.

---

[1] In Syriac, *pârshîn sh'mâ ðAlâhâ* : cf. Lev. xxiv 11.

21. "Let not the Periodeutæ, or the Priests or Deacons, stay in the public khans or in an inn when they enter the city, but let them stay in the Church's guest-house, or in the monasteries outside.

22. "Let Priests and Deacons and the Sons and Daughters of the Covenant abstain from wine and from flesh, but if there be any among them who is ill in body let him have a little, as it is written; but those who are drunken or who enter the wine-shops, let them be cast out of the Church.

23. "Let none of those who have become disciples of Christ be covetous to get more than their need, but let them act as stewards for the poor.

24-26. "Let not Priests and Deacons and Sons of the Covenant become keepers of threshing-floors or vineyards or the hired labourers of laymen, or bailiffs, or agents for laymen, or have anything to do with the law, but they are to keep to the Service of the Church and not to allow the offices of prayer and of psalm-singing to cease day or night."

The phrases about the law are rather obscure. Apparently the ecclesiastics were forbidden to become "sheriff's officers."

27. "Anathematise and bind and send to the city for judgment the laymen that dares to take to wife a Daughter of the Covenant; and if she also by her own consent was corrupted, let them send her also."

The tone of passion that still rings through this Canon makes me think that the contemplated event was likely to happen now and then, and that not a few of the Daughters of the Covenant repented of premature vows.

28. "Sons or Daughters of the Covenant that fall from their estate send to the monasteries for penance; but if they stay not in the monastery, let them not be received in the Church, except they be detained with their parents for so long a time as is right.

29. "Do not admit to instruction (or, 'discipleship') any woman that has a husband other than her own husband, nor any man that has a wife other than his lawful partner, that the Name of God be not blasphemed.

30. "Let not Priests permit those who are found in adultery to offer the Sacrament, save by our express permission.

31. "Let not any of the Priests or of the Deacons or any of the Sons of the Church dare to place common vessels side by side with the Sacramental vessels in any box or chest."

Here again we have the same tone of lofty indignation that we noticed with regard to appropriation of a Daughter of the Covenant, and it is only just to Rabbûla to observe that from his point of view he would regard it as exactly the same crime.

32. "Let no one dare to come near and give the Oblation, except he be a Priest or Deacon.

33. "All the lords of villages hold in the honour that is due to them, but not so that ye become servile and oppress the poor.

36. "Let them not permit the Sons of the Covenant to go to gatherings or other places except with Priests, nor the Daughters of the Covenant except with Deaconesses.

37. "Let not any one of the Priests or of the Deacons or of the Sons of the Covenant except by our command go

away to the Imperial Army (*Comitatus*) or to any distant place and leave his Church, even if it be a matter of business for his village or his Church.

38. "Let all the Priests take care for the service of the House of God, and let them be doing whatever is necessary for the ordering of the House, and let them not feed beasts in the Church, that the House of God be not brought into contempt.[1]

39. "The Periodeutes or Priest or Deacon that departs from this world, whatever he has he shall leave to the Church.

40. "Neither Priests nor Deacons nor Sons of the Covenant shall make themselves sureties for anyone, neither with or without a written deed.

41. "Let Priests and Deacons dwell in the Church, and if possible the Sons of the Covenant also.

42. "Let Priests and Deacons have a care that in all Churches a copy of the Separate Gospels (*Evangeliôn da-Mĕpharrĕshê*) shall be kept and used for reading.

43. "Let the Priests read the Gospel where there is a Priest, and not the Deacons; Baptism also where possible let Priests give.

44. "Let not Laymen be stewards in the Church, save where there are no Sons of the Covenant fit for the post.

45. "Let not Sons or Daughters of the Covenant drink wine at the funeral-feast (*lit.* 'after the defunct')."

This seems to have been regarded as a heathen rite.

47. "Let not the Sons of the Church have intercourse with heretics, neither in word or in deed.

---

[1] It is perhaps not out of place to mention that not a hundred years ago there was a Westmoreland Church, part of which was partitioned off as a fold for sheep. The parson sat in the Chancel spinning, while he taught the day-school.

THE CANONS OF RABBULA

49. "The books of heretics and their receptacles seek out in every place; and wherever ye can, either bring them to us or burn them in the fire.

51. "Let not Priests give the Oblation to those who are troubled with demons, that no disgrace befall the Sacrament in the Communion of devils.

56. "Let no man leave his wife, unless he has found her in adultery, nor let the wife leave her husband for all sorts of causes."

Note that it does not expressly say that these persons are assumed to be of the baptized: they may only be among those who had become "disciples of Christ" as in No. 23, *i.e.* unbaptized Catechumens.

57. "Let no man take to wife his sister's daughter or his brother's daughter, nor his father's sister or his mother's sister."

You will notice that the deceased wife's sister is not included in this simple Table of prohibited degrees. The Canons end with two further directions for the decent ordering of the Service, *viz*:

58. "Let not the Sons of the Covenant go up the altar-steps, or bring up any food into the apse; either let the Priest eat there, or let a man dine in the nave.[1] And let nothing be put there save the Sacramental vessels.

59. "Priests and Deacons when they give the Sacrament, let them not receive any gift from those that take the Sacrament."

---
[1] The Syriac is *nil'as b'haik'lâ*.

"Here end the commands and admonitions to Priests and Sons of the Covenant," says our document, and I think you will agree with me that they give us a very vivid picture of Syrian Church life in the fifth century. The *B'nai Q'yâmâ*, the Sons and Daughters of the Covenant, are still the backbone of the Church. They live separately in their own homes or in the homes of their near relations, or else in small informal communities such as the Clergy House sometimes attached to a large Anglican parish. Besides these there are "Disciples of Christ" who may be married, but it is not directly implied that these are in the enjoyment of the sacraments of the Church. It is very probable that by the time Rabbûla issued his Canons they were actually admitted to baptism and communion, but the ideal legislator does not always officially recognise lax customs that have sprung up: it would be a mistake to argue from the Anglican Bidding-Prayer that all the Commons of the realm were in sincere and conscientious communion with the Established Church.

I should have liked to conclude this Lecture by giving you an account of the introduction of the Marriage Service into the Syriac-speaking Church. But I have not been able to discover at what period this innovation was made. The Service actually adopted contained several picturesque features. There was a Benediction of the Wedding Rings, a Benediction of the Bridegroom and the Bride, a Benediction of their Wedding Crowns, and a Benediction of the Groomsmen.[1] No doubt a good deal of the ceremony is very ancient, and might afford material for students of sociology and of folk-lore. But what we are in search of is the introduction of a *religious* element into the feasting, the institution of *Holy Matrimony*. In the West of course it had been long practised, perhaps from the beginning, certainly from the time of Tertullian.[2] Among the Syriac-speaking branch of the Church, as we have seen, it was not a native growth.

I have devoted the whole of this Lecture to the one question of Christian Marriage, because the attitude of a religious institution toward matters of conduct and morality is after all more fundamentally important than its attitude to those high philosophical problems of theology which are only the pursuit of a few, however much the party watchwords may become the battle cries of the many. And we may well rejoice

---

[1] To be found *e.g.* in B.M. Add. 14493, a MS. of the tenth century.
[2] *Felicitatem eius matrimonii quod . . . . obsignat benedictio* (Tert. *ad Vxorem* ii 8).

that the tendency which developed in the early Syriac-speaking branch of the Church more strongly than elsewhere failed to become the established law. The solemnization of weddings by a Christian rite is a custom so familiar to us, that we may easily come to think of it as natural and inevitable, but the words of Aphraates teach us that it was not always so regarded. We cannot doubt that he would have regarded such a ceremony with horror.

The healthier instinct of the West has saved us from a Buddhistic organisation of Christendom, for it is surely no light gain to Christian society that the bridal feast has been hallowed with the blessing of the Church. "Holy religion of matrimony should men and women be taught of priests by authority of God's law, and then when they take it they would be the more able to keep it virtuously. . . . For through his children a man is known, faithful or unfaithful; faithful if he keep the honest religion of wedlock as is before said, and unfaithful if he do the contrary." These words from an unknown Lollard commentator on the Psalms[1] express far more nearly than anything I have read to you from Aphraates or Rabbûla

---

[1] Quoted by Miss A. C. Paues (from B. M. Reg. 18 C 26, *f.* 146) in *A Fourteenth Century English Biblical Version*, p. xlix.

THE BRIDES OF CHRIST

a worthy Christian view of man and wife and of their duties to themselves and to society.

In conclusion I must remind you of the immense part played, both in the discouragement of marriage and in its subsequent permission, by the doctrine of the Sacraments. According to Aphraates, strict continence is the way to secure the physical efficiency of Baptism for a good resurrection on the last day.[1] And he uses with pleasure the unfortunate metaphor of the Brides of Christ, who in place of a mortal husband are betrothed to the Messiah.[2] The same tone of reprobation is used by Rabbûla for the man who marries a Daughter of the Covenant, with or without her consent, and for the man who puts ordinary objects in the same box with the sacramental furniture: both crimes are an act of sacrilege against the Vessels in which Christ is pleased locally to dwell. The way of Life, that is to say the method of obtaining life in the next world, was through the Sacraments; and when this view was clearly conceived, the first answer of the Christian community in the flush of its early enthusiasm was that so sacred a means must be honoured in those who use it by a special manner of living. This answered

---

[1] Aphraates, *Wright* 125, *Gwynn* 372.
[2] *Wright* 115 *f*, *Gwynn* 367 *f*.

well enough for the needs of the Church while it was a comparatively small and persecuted body, but the time came when all the world wished to be at least nominally Christian, and a change was inevitable. The way of Life, they said, is through the Sacraments. Without the Sacraments we are doomed to eternal misery: therefore the way of living to be required from baptized Christians must be something compatible with ordinary life in the world. Those who wished for the protection of the Sacraments all their life obviously could not promise to be monks and nuns, and so the great change came about. The interest of the Syriac-speaking Church for the study of the evolution of the Christian society lies in this, that in it this great change was not completed till the fifth century A.D.

EDESSA.
View looking W.N.W.

[To face p. 155.

LECTURE V

BARDAISAN AND HIS DISCIPLES

As Renan said long ago, and as William Wright repeats in the opening words of his Short History of Syriac Literature, the characteristic of the Syrians is a certain mediocrity. They shone neither in war, nor in the arts, nor in science. They lacked the poetic fire of the older Hebrews and of the Arabs. But they were apt enough as pupils of the Greeks; they assimilated and reproduced, adding little or nothing of their own. There was no *Alfarabi*, no *Avicenna*, no *Averroës*, in the cloisters of Edessa, Qinnesrîn, or Nisibis. The Syrian Church of the fourth and succeeding centuries failed to produce men who rose to the level of a Eusebius, a Gregory Nazianzen, a Basil, and a Chrysostom. "The literature of Syria," says Dr Wright, "is, on the whole, not an attractive one." I am not going to challenge this severe verdict on the general ground. Syriac Literature presents the depressing spectacle of a steady Decline and

Fall, following the general collapse of civilisation in the East. Moreover what we have of it is a specialised department. The Syriac Literature that has come down to us is not, like the literature of the Greeks or Arabs, a selection of almost all the departments of human activity. What we have in Syriac is practically nothing more than the contents of a very fine monastic Library. Many departments of profane literature are but little represented and even the ancient heretics are rarely allowed to speak to us, except through the imperfect medium of orthodox refutations.

What we have of Syriac Literature is, taken in the lump, dull. But there are some indications that outside the walls of the orthodox cloisters there was in early times some independent life and light, and a little has percolated through to us. I propose in the present Lecture to illustrate this side of Syriac Literature from the one philosophical work of the School of Bardaisan that has come down to us.

Bardaisan, called "The last of the Gnostics," a man distinguished by birth, by learning, by intelligence, became a Christian during the last quarter of the second century. He died in the year 222 A.D., having by that time separated himself from the organisation of the Church of his native place. Later ages regarded him as

THE LAST OF THE GNOSTICS

a heretic; and when the sect that had been formed by his followers died out, the monastic libraries did not greatly care to preserve even the orthodox confutations of his doctrine. We are therefore obliged to reconstruct from scattered notices and the ill-informed partisan statements of later chroniclers our picture of the only original thinker which the Syriac Church helped to mould.

Let us first hear what Eusebius has to tell us, writing barely a century after the death of Bardaisan. Eusebius (*HE* iv 30) says that Bardesanes (as the Greeks called *Bardaiṣân*) was a most competent writer in his native Syriac, and that he wrote treatises against Marcion and other heretics, some of which had been translated into Greek. Among these was a Dialogue on Fate addressed to "Antoninus," by whom Eusebius (or his source) may have meant Caracalla, or even Elagabalus. We are told further that Bardesanes had been a disciple of Valentinus the Gnostic, but that he abandoned his teaching for more orthodox views, yet without ever quite shaking off the old slough of heretical opinion. Eusebius gives no exact dates, but puts Bardaisan under Pope Soter, *i.e.* about 179, the traditional date of his conversion to Christianity.

Epiphanius tells us more, but as usual it is not safe to trust all that this amiable Father of the Church says about a heretic. He evidently regarded the accession of Bardaisan to Christianity as one of the results of the conversion of the blessed King Abgar. He seems however to have some knowledge of Bardaisan's works, for he tells us quite truly that the Dialogue on Fate was written against the doctrines of a certain 'Awîda the Astrologer.[1] But whereas Eusebius tells us that Bardaisan had been a follower of Valentinus and never quite shook off his heresy, Epiphanius makes him become a follower of Valentinus after he had been orthodox.

The fullest account of Bardaisan is that inserted in the Syriac Chronicle of Michael the Great, Jacobite Patriarch of Antioch from 1166 to 1199. We have already had occasion to discuss this account in the first of these Lectures when considering the early episcopal succession to the See of Edessa, but it may not be out of place to remind you once again how circumspect we ought to be in trusting to details preserved in so late a source. Bardaisan lived a thousand years before the Patriarch Michael compiled his Chronicle, and we can only regard the Chronicle

---
[1] Αὐειδὰν τὸν ἀστρονόμον (*Oehler* i, pt. 2, p. 144, note).

as a serious source of historical information in those passages where there is good reason to believe that Michael and his predecessors have all copied faithfully from a much older source. In the present case we have to allow for ignorance and prejudice: ignorance, because the learning and the philosophy of an independent thinker are not easily packed into the compendiums of annalists, and prejudice, because Bardaisan's name was chiefly known in later ages as that of a great heretic and schismatic, and it was assumed that he must have been immoral and irrational. With these reservations let us take Michael's account.

After declaring how Bardaisan was converted in 179 A.D. by Bishop Hystasp of Edessa, and ordained by him a Deacon (!)[1] Michael mentions that Bardaisan wrote treatises against heresies and that he turned to the doctrines of Valentinus. He then goes on to tell us: "Bardaisan says that there are three chief Natures (*K'yânê*) and four existences (*Îthyê*), which are Reason and Power and Understanding and Knowledge. The four Powers are Fire and Water and Light and Spirit (or Wind), and from these come the other existences of the world[2] to the number

---

[1] Chabot, *Michel le Syrien* [110].
[2] The MS. has "and the world."

of 360. And Bardaisan says that He who spake with Moses and the Prophets was the Chief of the Angels and not God Himself; our Lord was clothed with the body of an Angel and [from][1] Mary the shining Soul was clothed which thus took form and body. Furthermore the Upper Powers gave man his soul and the Lower Powers gave him his limbs: the Sun gave the brain, and the Moon and the Planets gave the other parts." Then follow some almost unintelligible remarks about the syzygy of the Sun and Moon, whereby the material world is renewed every month. Michael then informs us that according to Bardaisan "the Messiah, the Son of God, was born under the planet Jupiter, crucified in the hour of Mars, buried in the hour of Mercury, and in the time of Jupiter He arose from the grave." Bardaisan also said that the dead do not rise and that dreams are true, and marriage he calls a good purification.[2] He had three sons, Abgarôn, Hasdu, and Harmonius, who all remained true to his doctrines.

It is difficult to extract from this confused farrago of statements anything certain about

---

[1] The MS. omits "from."
[2] So Bar Hebraeus understands the passage from which Michael quotes.

the real nature of Bardaisan's teaching. At the same time some of the statements above quoted are confirmed from other sources, such as the express declaration in Ephraim's Treatise against False Doctrines (*Ad Hypatium*, bk. ii, in *Overbeck*, p. 63) that Bardaisan had said that the human Soul was mixed and compounded of seven constituents. Unfortunately the latter part of this valuable prose Treatise exists only as an almost illegible palimpsest which still awaits a decipherer.[1] The metrical discourses of Ephraim against Heretics must also be used with great caution, for the very reason that they are written in metre. It is difficult to quote one's adversary accurately, if you are tied down to a verse of five syllables to the line.

Fortunately we are not entirely obliged to gain our knowledge of Bardaisan from refutations of his opinions. The *Dialogue on Fate*, mentioned by Eusebius and Epiphanius, has been actually preserved. Like so many other treasures of Syriac literature it was discovered

---

[1] What Overbeck has published is only the First Book and about half the Second There were originally Five Books, each beginning in turn with the five letters of Ephraim's name (A F R Y M). The palimpsest mentioned in the text is B.M. Add. 14623.

by Dr Cureton, when Keeper of the Oriental MSS. at the British Museum and also Rector of this Church of S. Margaret's, Westminster.

A surprise meets us at the outset. This famous Dialogue, mentioned by several Fathers in a Greek translation, and actually in large part incorporated into more than one ancient Christian writing, does not profess to be the work of Bardaisan, but of his disciple Philip. Bardaisan himself is the chief speaker and teaches with authority, but Philip writes in the first person. This Philip is otherwise entirely unknown, and the name, so common in Greek, is rarely met with among the Syrians. Thus the suspicion arises whether he is anything more than a literary device. In any case there is no reason to suppose that there is any analogy between the parts played by Bardaisan and Philip in the *De Fato* with those of Socrates and Plato in the Platonic Dialogues. A truer literary analogy would be found between S. Paul and that Tertius who wrote the Epistle to the Romans.

A further formal difficulty is to be found in the name of the Dialogue. The Greek writers who know of it speak of it as a treatise *On Fate*, a very suitable description. But the Syriac MS. is headed, "The Book of the Laws of Countries,"

AUTHORSHIP OF THE DIALOGUE

and some modern writers have assumed that this is the true title. I incline however to believe that the Greeks were right, and that the Syriac heading of our MS. is not so much the original title as an indication of the cause of its preservation. It is inconceivable that a work of the heresiarch Bardaisan or of his immediate disciples should have been intentionally preserved except on a side issue. A side issue is actually provided by the interesting descriptions of heathen customs and laws mentioned at the end of the Dialogue. The customs are curious reading in themselves and they are mentioned in illustration of the disciplinary power of Christianity. For the sake of the mention of these customs the Dialogue was valued in later times, and from the description of them it acquired this name of the "Book of the Laws of Countries." But the work as a whole is really about Fate, and it is more appropriate to continue to call it the Dialogue *On Fate*.

The Dialogue opens with narrative: whoever "Philip" may have been, he was certainly master of a pleasant style and the art of arranging his material. "A few days ago," he says, "we went in to pay a call on our brother Shamshagram, and there Bardaisan came and found us; and when he had inquired and found him well, he asked us what we were talking about, 'for,' said he, 'I heard the sound of your conversation outside when I was coming in.' For it was his custom, whenever he found us talking, to ask us what it was about, that he might speak thereon with us. And we said to him: 'Awida here was saying to us, "If God is one, as you say, and He constituted the race of men, and really wills what you are commanded to do, why did He not constitute them so that they could not go wrong, but always do what is good? For in that case His will would be done."'"

The problem is not exactly a new one, but even after many centuries the solution is not in our hands. Let us see how this school of Christian Philosophers looked at the question.

Bardaisan first replies: "Tell me, my son Awida, do you mean that there is not One who is God over all, or do you mean that the One God does not intend that men should conduct themselves justly and rightly?" Awida answers that he asked his friends to see what they would say first, as he was shy of asking Bardaisan himself. Bardaisan assures him that those who come with a sincere desire to learn the truth and to set forth genuinely felt difficulties have no reason to be shy; it is the duty of the Master to attempt to answer such difficulties when they are put forth. Awida then says that his difficulties are genuinely his own, but that Bardaisan's disciples would not persuade him by arguments and kept saying, "you have only to believe and you will be able to know everything," and Awida on the other hand said that he could not believe, except he was shown reason for doing so.

Here we approach the real teaching of the Dialogue. Bardaisan does not reply directly to Awida, but turns to his own disciples, saying: "It is not Awida alone who does not wish to believe. Many others are in the same case, and because there is no faith in them they cannot be shown reason, but they are continually pulling down and building up, and the end is a mere shapeless ruin in which knowledge of truth cannot dwell. But (he continues) since Awida says he does not wish to believe, I will talk to you that do believe about the question which he has asked, and thus he may hear something more." So Bardaisan begins to say: "Many men there are who from lack of faith have difficulty even in listening to instruction, because they have no foundation to build on and are even in doubt about God Himself. Such men have not that Fear of God which delivers us from all fears, but are at the same time timid and rash. Now as to the question that Awida asks, why God has not made us so that we could not sin and so not be guilty before Him, I reply that if man had been so made he would not be himself, but a machine. Man would be like a harp on which the performer plays: the praise and the blame, and even the very knowledge of how the instrument is being used, belong to the musician and not to the harp. But God in His kindness did not wish to make man thus, and so He endowed men with much greater freedom than many things, equal in fact with the angels. For look (said he) at the Sun and the Moon and the Planets, and all the rest of those things which are so much greater than we in some respects: to these freedom in themselves has not been given, but they are all so fixed that they can only move in the path marked out for them. The Sun cannot say, 'I will not appear at the right time,' the Moon cannot say, 'I will not wax and wane,' the Stars must rise and set when they are due, the Sea cannot help carrying the ships, the Mountains and the Earth cannot help remaining each in its place; for all these things are mere vehicles of the Wisdom of God that never goes wrong. If everything was only formed to be useful for something else, for whose benefit would the world be made? And if everything was only formed to receive benefits, how would the service of the world be supplied? As it is, no things are wholly detached one from the other; for an absolutely self-contained power or thing would be an Element which has not yet received its place in the organisation of the universe. The things needed for human use have been placed within the sphere of human activity. This is what is meant when we read in Genesis that man was made in the image of God. Out of the Divine Kindness it was given to man that the things needful for his life should be his servants during this present dispensation, and that he should conduct himself as he pleases. What is in his power to do, he can do if he pleases, and can leave undone if he pleases. He can, in a word, control himself or fail to control himself, and the praise or blame which his conduct deserves is really his own. See then (continues Bardaisan) how greatly the goodness of God has been exercised towards men, in that so much more freedom has been given to man than to other things, that by means of it he may control himself, and so act the part of God and be reckoned with the Angels. For Angels also have freedom such as men have, as we may see from the story in Genesis of those Sons of God who mingled themselves with the daughters of men. Had they not done this they would not have fallen from their exalted station and received their due need of punishment; and similarly we may infer that those which did not fall thus, but kept control of themselves when exposed to temptation, were exalted and hallowed and became the recipients of great gifts. For every being that exists has need of the Lord of all, and to His gifts there is no end; yet know this (says Bardaisan), that even those things which are governed by fixed laws, as I said, are nevertheless not entirely deprived of all freedom, and therefore at the last all of them are subject to Judgment."

Then I said: "And how are those things judged whose movements are fixed beforehand?"

He saith to me: "The powers of Nature, O Philip, are not judged in respect of what they have been *made* to do, but in respect of what they have been *entrusted* to do. For the Elements are not deprived of their nature when they are assigned their place in the Universe, but the vehemence of their peculiar properties is lessened by the mixture of one with the other, and moreover they are under subjection to the power of Him who made them. Yet in so far as they are in subjection they are not brought to judgment, but only in respect of what is in their own power."

After this Awida says to Bardaisan: "All this that you have said is excellent, but how strict are the commandments that have been given to men! They cannot be performed."

Bardaisan replied: "This is the utterance of one who does not really wish to do what is good, one who obeys the Enemy of man and is subject to him. For nothing has been commanded to men but what they are able to do. There are two commandments set before us, very fit and proper exercises for our free nature: the one is, that we should abstain from everything that is evil and that we hate to be done to us, and the other, that we should do what is good and what we like to be done to us. For what man is physically unable to keep from stealing or lying or adultery or malicious false witness? All these things belong to the mind of man, to his disposition, not to his material lot. Even if a man be poor or diseased or old or crippled he can abstain from doing these evil deeds; and just as he can abstain from these things, so also he can love and bless and speak truth and pray for the welfare of everyone he knows. And if he be well and have the opportunity of giving something of his own, he can do so; he can use the material force at his command for the support of the weak. There is no one who cannot do this. In fact, the Commandments of God are concerned with those very matters which are within the range of human control. We are not commanded to carry heavy burdens of stone or wood or anything else, which only those who are strong of body are able to do;[1] nor to build towns and found cities, which only kings are able to do; nor to steer ships, which only sailors have skill to manage; nor to survey land and divide it, which only surveyors know how to do; nor to practise any other of the arts, which some can do and the rest are shut out from. To us through God's kindness such equable commandments have been given as every living man can do with pleasure; for there is no one who does not rejoice when he is doing well, and no one who keeps himself from doing hateful deeds who

---

[1] The same argument is curiously repeated in the Acts of Thomas (*Wright* 253; E. Trans., p. 219): "For we are not commanded to do anything which we are unable to do, nor to take up heavy burdens, nor to build buildings, which carpenters build for themselves with wisdom, nor to practise the art of hewing stones, which stone-cutters know as their craft; but we are commanded to do something which we can do,—to refrain from fornication, the head of all evils, and from murder, etc." The ethical theory is the same, and I venture to suggest that both 'Philip' and the author of the *Acts of Thomas* derived it from Bardaisan. The question is important to us from its bearing on the authorship of the *Hymn of the Soul*. See p. 199.

does not feel at ease in himself—except indeed those who have not been created for good and who are called Tares. For the Judge of all is not so unjust as to blame man for what he cannot do."

Awida then said: "Do you say of these things, O Bardaisan, that they are easy to do?"

Bardaisan replies: "To him that *wishes* to do them I said, and still say, that they are easy, for they are the appropriate course for the mind of a free man to take and for a soul that has not rebelled against those who control it. But in bodily activities many things interfere with the ideal course, especially old age and sickness and poverty."

Awida says: "Perhaps one may keep from doing wrong, but who among men is able to do good?"

This Bardaisan denies, declaring that doing good is the natural action of man, while doing evil is really unnatural and the work of the Enemy; evil, in fact, is a disease. To do good gives real pleasure; the pleasure we may get from evil is as different from this as the quiet that comes from exhaustion and despair differs from the quiet we get in health. Desire is one thing, Love is another; Christian charity is not mere good-fellowship. "The counterfeit of Love is Desire. Desire may have satisfaction for an hour, but it is far from being true Love, whose satisfaction has neither corruption nor dissolution for ever."

The writer of the Dialogue then remarks: "Awida was saying that men do wrong from their nature: if men had not been designed to do wrong, they would not do wrong."

Bardaisan says: "If all men acted the same way, and had only one set of opinions, we should conclude that their actions were the result of their nature, and that they had no freedom such as I have been describing to you. But that you may understand what is Nature and what is Freedom, I shall go on to point out to you that the Nature of man is to be born, to grow up, to arrive at full age, to beget and to grow old, eating and drinking, sleeping and waking, and finally to die. These things, because they are part of the Nature of man, belong to all men; and not to men only, but also to everything that has life, in fact, some of them are shared even by plants. This belongs to the sphere of the physical constitution of everything, whereby it is made, created, and set in the world, each according to its own laws. Furthermore we find the laws of Nature are uniformly observed by the various animals. The lion eats meat by Nature, and therefore all lions are eaters of meat; the sheep eats grass by Nature, and therefore all sheep are eaters of grass. All bees, all ants, store up food for themselves in the same way; all scorpions are ready to sting without being attacked. All the animals keep their own laws: the eaters of flesh do not become eaters of grass, nor do the eaters of grass become eaters of flesh.

"But men do not behave in this way. In the affairs of their bodies they keep the laws of their nature like beasts, but in the affairs of their minds they do what they will, acting as if they were free or at least entrusted with freedom, after the image of God. For some of them eat meat and no bread, some of them distinguish between various sorts of foods, and some of them eat nothing that has had in it the breath of life. There are some who have intercourse with their mothers, their sisters, and their daughters; others keep altogether from women. There are some who are fierce as lions and leopards; and some who hurt those who have done them no wrong, like the scorpion; and some that are driven like sheep and do no harm to those that drag them along. Some act with kindness, some with justice, some with malice; and if any one say that he is only acting in accordance with his Nature, a little reflection will show that this is not the case. For there are some who used to be adulterers and drunkards, but when a discipline of good counsel reached them they have become modest and temperate, and have despised the desire of their bodies; and there are some who used to live modestly and temperately, but when they neglected right discipline, they have resisted the commands of God and of their teachers, have fallen from the way of truth and have become adulterers and prodigals. And some have repented again, and have returned in fear to the truth in which they stood. Which, then, is the Nature of man? For lo, they are all different one from the other in their way of life and in their desires, and they that hold in a certain opinion and way of thinking resemble each other in their ways. Nevertheless, men who as yet are subject to the enticements of their desires and are led by their passions wish to lay the faults they commit at the door of their Maker, so that they may be considered faultless themselves. The moral law does not apply to that which belongs to Nature: no one is to be blamed for being tall or short, or white or black, or for any bodily defect, but a man deserves blame for thieving or lying or cursing and such like. Whence it may be seen that for the things which are not in our power, but come to us from Nature, we are not held guilty, nor can we control them; but for the things that belong to our freedom, if we do well the verdict is for us and we are deserving of praise, while if we do evil we are guilty and deserve blame."

At this point of the Dialogue comes in the famous disquisition on Fate. "We asked him," says Philip, "whether there are not some who say that men are controlled by the decrees of Fate, sometimes in an evil direction, sometimes in a good direction."

Bardaisan replies: "I well know, O Philip, that some of those men who are called Chaldæans, and others also, have a love for this very knowledge of the Art, as I also once had myself, for it has been said by me elsewhere that the mind of man yearns to know what most folk do not know, and this these persons think they do, holding that all the faults they commit and all the good they do and all that befalls them in wealth and in poverty, in sickness and in health and in bodily injury, come to them from the action of the so-called Seven Stars or Planets, and are controlled by their motions. There are others who say in opposition to these either that this Art is all a lie of the Chaldæans or that there is no such thing as Fate, and that all things both great and small are really in men's own power, and that diseases and bodily defects are mere matters of chance. Others again say that everything a man does he does of his own will through the Freedom given to him, and that defects and diseases and other misfortunes which befall are a punishment from God. Now in my humble opinion (says Bardaisan), it seems to me that these three opinions have each of them something that is true and something that is false. They are true, inasmuch as men speak according to what they actually see around them, and we cannot help noticing how things turn out adversely against us; but they are false, inasmuch as the Wisdom of God is richer than they, that Wisdom which established the worlds and created man and appointed the rulers of the various powers of the Universe, and gave to all things a responsibility suitable to each one of them. For I say that the authority possessed by the various orders of the Universe of which I have spoken —Gods,[1] Angels, Authorities, Celestial Rulers, Elements, Men, and Beasts—the authority given to each and all of them is partial. There is only One who has universal authority. But the others have authority in some matters and not in others, as I have already said; that in so far as they have authority the kindness of God may appear,

---

[1] Evidently we should read *alâhê*, in the plural.

and in so far as they have no authority they may know that they have a supreme Lord.

"There is therefore such a thing as Fate, as the Chaldæans say. But that not everything happens according to our will is obvious from this, that most men desire to be rich and powerful and healthy and successful, and as a matter of fact only a few are so, and that not completely nor during all their life. Some have children and cannot rear them, some rear them only to prove a disgrace and a sorrow. Moreover men are not equally fortunate in all things; one man is rich as he likes to be, but unhealthy as he does not like to be, and another is healthy as he likes to be, but poor as he does not like to be. Some have many things they want and a few things they do not want, and some have a few things they want and many things they do not want. And thus we see that wealth and honours and health and sickness and children, and the various objects of desire are placed under Fate and not under our authority; but in the case of such of these things as happen according to our wish we accept them willingly and are pleased, and when they happen against our wish we are compelled to accept them whether we like or no. From the things which happen to us against our wish we see how it really stands with what we do wish : it is not because we will them that we get them, but they happen as they happen, and with some of the things we are pleased and with some of them not. And so we men are found to be governed by Nature equally, by Fate diversely, and by our Freedom as each man likes.

"But now we will go on to show that Fate and its dominion does not extend over everything. What we call 'Fate' is really the arrangement of the course marked out to the heavenly Powers and to the Elements by God. According to this arrangement the various faculties are assorted as they come down into the soul and the various souls are assorted as they come down into the bodies, and the agency by which this sorting is done is called the Fate and the Nativity of the congeries out of which the individual is evolved, all to help on that design which God in His mercy and grace has deigned to help and continues to do so until the consummation of all things.

"The body therefore is governed by Nature, and the soul suffers and perceives with it, and Fate cannot help or hinder the body against its Nature. Fate cannot give a man or woman children at a time when they are too young or too old by Nature to have children. Nor can Fate keep a man's body alive without eating and drinking, nor even when a man has food and drink can Fate keep a man so that he shall not die, for these and many other things belong to Nature. But when the conditions of Nature are complied with, within this limited field Fate comes into play, and it makes things to differ one with the other, sometimes helping and sometimes hindering the ordinary operation of Nature. Thus from Nature comes the growth of the body and its arrival at maturity, but apart from Nature and by Fate come sicknesses and defects in the body. From Nature comes the natural inclination of man and woman, but from Fate comes repugnance and also unnatural lusts. From Nature comes birth and children, but from Fate comes miscarriage and other failures. From Nature there is sufficiency in moderation for all, but from Fate comes on the one hand need and distress for food, and on the other extravagance and unnecessary luxury. Nature requires that elders should be the judges of youths, and wise men of fools, and that the strong should rule the weak and brave men command cowards; but Fate makes children to be the chiefs of elders and fools the chiefs of wise men, and that in time of war weak men command the strong and cowards command the brave. Know this especially (continued Bardaisan), that whenever the course of Nature is disturbed, the disturbance comes from this that I call Fate; and the reason of it is that the various Powers over which Fate is set are contrary one to the other, and some of them —those which we say are on the *right* hand —help Nature and add to its beauty, when the course of things is in their favour and they are in the ascendant in the heavenly Sphere, in their own portions; while others—which we say are on the *left*—are malignant, and when they are in the ascendant they are opposed to Nature, and they injure not men only, but beasts and plants and crops from time to time, as well as the seasons and fountains of water, everything, in fact, that is in Nature which is under their control. And it is because of these divisions and contrarieties between the Powers that some men have supposed that the world is governed without Providence, because they do not know that this contrariety and division of the Powers and their consequent conquest and defeat are the result of the free constitution that was given them from God, that these created things also by their own delegated powers might either conquer or be defeated.

"As we have seen that Fate destroys the work of Nature, so may we see the Freedom of man repelling Fate and destroying its work; yet not in everything, just as Fate cannot in everything repel Nature. For these three things, Nature, Fate and Freedom, must be kept in being, until the appointed course be fulfilled and the measure and the number of the days be accomplished, and all Beings and Natures have had their full existence."

Here Bardaisan stops for a moment, having come to a pause in his description of the forces by which all individuals are swayed. According to him, Nature determines the general conditions of each individual's existence, Fate determines the career, while the Freedom (or, as we say, the Free-will) of the individual is chiefly active in determining his character.

Awida now begins to be persuaded. He confesses himself satisfied that it is not from Nature that a man does wrong, and he sees that all men are not equally subjected to the same influences. Now he asks if it can be proved that it is not from Fate that men do wrong. "If this can be shown," he says, "we must believe that a man really possesses Freedom, and that by Nature he is brought to what is good and warned against what is bad;

and so he is justly liable to judgment at the last day."

Bardaisan replies: "From the fact that all men are not equally subjected to the same influences you are persuaded that it is not from their common Nature that men do wrong. Well then, you will be obliged to agree that it is not entirely from their Fate that they act wrongly if we can show you that the decree of the Fates and Powers do not equally affect all men, but that we really have some Freedom in ourselves not to serve physical Nature and not to be moved by the control of the heavenly Powers."

Awida says: "Show me this and I will believe and do whatever you tell me."

The reply of Bardaisan was in ancient times the most famous part of the whole Dialogue, and in a Greek dress it was borrowed wholesale by Eusebius and by the author of the *Clementine Recognitions*. But we need not linger very long over its curious erudition, except so far as concerns his descriptions of the "new race" of Christians. Speaking as an astrologer to an astrologer, Bardaisan reminds Awida that according to the rules of the Art each individual's Fate follows from the configuration of the heavenly bodies at the time of birth. But he runs through the nations of the earth

THE VARIED CUSTOMS OF NATIONS

from the Chinese on the east to the Britons on the west. Each nation has its own customs of marriage, of social life, of morals. But the inhabitants of these various countries are not all born at the same time, at the same configuration of the heavens. It is therefore not their Fate that compels the several nations each to keep their own customs and to avoid those of other people. For instance, says Bardaisan, in the whole of Media all men when they die, even while life is still remaining in them, are cast to the dogs and the dogs eat the dead of the whole of Media;[1] but we cannot say that all the Medians are born when the Moon is in conjunction with Mars in the constellation Cancer during the day below the Earth, as ought to be the case by the rules of Astrology for those who are to be eaten by dogs. The varied customs of the people of the earth prove that Fate does not act in the mechanical way that the Astrologers believe: the customs of the various countries, whether indigenous or forced upon the inhabitants by foreign rulers, are the result of human Free-will and are not

---

[1] See *Strabo* xi 517, quoted by E. R. Bevan, *House of Seleucus* i 290. The reason of the custom was of course to prevent the sacred elements of Earth, Air, Fire, and Water, from being polluted by a dead body.

due to the operations of Fate. It was not Fate, but the decree of King Abgar when he was converted to Christianity, that stopped the people of Edessa from mutilating themselves in honour of Atargatis. And so Bardaisan comes at last to his own Church.

"What then," he says, "shall we say of the new race of us Christians, whom in every country and in every region the Messiah established at His coming? For lo, all of us wherever we be are called Christians by the one Name of the Messiah; and on one day, the first of the week, we assemble together, and on specified days we abstain from food. And of these national customs, our brethren abstain from all that are contrary to their profession. Parthian Christians do not take two wives, Jewish Christians are not circumcised. Our sisters among the Bactrians do not practise promiscuity with strangers. Our Persian brethren do not take their daughters to wife; our Median brethren do not desert their dying relatives or bury them alive or throw them to the dogs. Nor do Christians in Edessa kill their wives or sisters that commit fornication, as the heathen Edessenes do, but they keep apart from them and commit them to the judgment of God. Nor do Christians in

Ḥatra stone thieves. But in whatever place they are, neither do the national laws separate them from the Law of the Messiah, nor does the Fate arranged by the Powers compel them to make use of what is impure to them. Yet sickness and health, and riches and poverty, matters that are not within their Free-will, these befall them wherever they are. For as the Free-will of men is not regularly governed by the compulsion of the Seven Planets, and even when so governed is able to withstand them, so also it remains true that man as we see him cannot easily get free from the orders of his governing influences, for he is a slave and put in subjection.

"To sum up, if we were really free to do everything, we should be everything; and if we were wholly without power to act, we should be mere machines in the hand of others. But when God so wills, everything can happen without disturbance, for His great and holy Will nothing can hinder. Those who think they can resist are in a position not of strength, but of evil and of error, and such a position may stand for a short time, because He is kind and permits all Natures to stand where they do and to be governed by their own will, yet bound by what has been done and by the constitution of things that was made for their help. For by the order and governance that has been given to things and the mixture of one principle with another the vehemence of the various Natures is weakened, so that they do not altogether injure nor are they altogether injured, as they used to injure and be injured before the creation of the world. And there will come a time when this power of injury which still subsists in them will be brought to an end through the doctrine which is coming to pass at the new mixture. And in the establishment of that new world, all the evil motions will cease and all rebellions will come to an end; the foolish will be persuaded and deficiencies will be filled up, and there will be peace and tranquillity by the gift of Him who is Lord of all Natures."

In this long abstract of the argument of the *De Fato* I have purposely given a very free translation, or rather paraphrase, because our object has been to follow the thought more than the actual language. It is difficult to realise how an ancient work of this kind appeals to other people; but to myself, coming from the study of ordinary Syriac ecclesiastical literature, the first impression made is of the independence of the writer's mind. It gives me the impression of being the thoughts of one who had learned to think for himself, one who had read much and thought much, and who was not content at the end merely to repeat the formulas of a school. Bardaisan brings out of the storehouse of his learning things new and old, and his imagination has woven them into a new and independent pattern. Such work is of a different order from that of men whose whole achievement is to reproduce as much of the philosophy of someone else — of Aristotle or of Proclus —as they have been able to understand.

The next reflexion of the student of ecclesiastical history will be that the Syriac-speaking Church was not able to retain Bardaisan in its communion. You have heard the argument of the *De Fato*, and you are in a position to appreciate the ideas which the School of Bardaisan cherished "on God, on Nature, and on human Life." That the *De Fato* really comes from the School of Bardaisan is certain, whether or no Bardaisan had a share in the actual literary composition of it; and I am quite sure that it gives a far truer picture of the spirit which animated Bardaisan and his disciples than the spiteful polemic of S. Ephraim or the unintelligently repeated catchwords which are echoed by various late chroniclers. But in that case we must feel it a pity that the Church made Bardaisan into a heretic. The whole Dialogue is pervaded by an admirable spirit. It is marked by reverence towards the Lord of all things and by gratitude for His benefits, by cheerful obedience to the ordinary discipline of the Church, by courtesy towards opponents, and above all by a firm faith that the Judge of all the earth will not do injustice. Less admirable perhaps from the narrower ecclesiastical standpoint is the firm and clear determination not to do violence to the facts of nature and of life. The writer refuses to shut his eyes to what he sees around him at the bidding of a theory, and his field of vision was not limited to Church History and the Old Testament. It was doubtless Bardaisan's independence of mind that led to his excommunication. We dare not press the details of the story of how Bishop 'Aqai "warned" him, but it is easy to imagine the scene. We may fancy the difficulties which Bardaisan's learned theories may have caused when caught up by ignorant brethren. We may fancy the bishop waiting on the philosopher, a man great both by birth and by achievement, and requesting him to modify his views. May we not go on to imagine that Bardaisan heard him out, listening at first with amused courtesy, and then when the Churchman proved deaf alike to explanation and to reasoning, accepting without much searching of heart the sentence of ostracism from the Christians' conventicle? This is mere fancy; but in sober fact it was a regrettable incident. We know next to nothing of the history of the School of Bardaisan, save that Rabbûla induced the remaining members to submit to the Church, some century and a quarter after. By that time the mischief had been done. We can see how grievously the Syriac-speaking Church suffered by failure to attract and to bear with the best scientific intellect of the time. It is a foolish and cowardly policy for a Church to be tolerant to superstition and rigid towards reverent speculation. The Syriac-speaking Church ultimately sank into formal heresies, while the great mass of the populations of the East adopted the new faith of Islam; I cannot help wondering how much of the collapse may have had its roots in intellectual cowardice.

Life and progress mean change, the rejection of what is worn-out or unsuitable as well as mere development; the mere "keeping one's wicket up," to adopt the phrase championed by the Bishop of Worcester, can only issue in stagnation. And the story of Bardaisan is being enacted over again just outside our own doors. It has been impossible to study Bardaisan's career without thinking of the case of the Abbé Loisy. The parallel is all the closer if there be anything in the tradition which puts Bardaisan into Holy Orders. Moreover, both writers are known for their treatises against heretics: Bardaisan wrote against Marcion and *l'Évangile et l'Église* is a defence of the Catholic Church against the Protestantism of Dr Harnack. But the inner resemblance is independent of these external circumstances. The essential point of resemblance is that M. Loisy, like Bardaisan, takes account of the Science which exists outside the narrow bounds of ecclesiastical study. He recognises its validity and its claim to judge those portions of ecclesiastical tradition which lie within its own sphere. To recognise this is to recognise that part of the traditional presentation of Christianity and part of its traditional defences must be modified from time to time if we are to retain the chief point, namely that our philosophy of religion shall be firmly based on observed facts and not erected on a flimsy scaffolding to correspond with some ideal plane, a scaffolding liable to collapse when the supports are removed or undermined. Bardaisan was declared a heretic, M. Loisy has been condemned by the Holy Office; may the intellectual paralysis which overspread the Syriac Churches be averted from our own Church and the Church of Rome!

There is one thing in conclusion upon which I should be glad to lay stress. The Dialogue *On Fate* is in form a dispute between a Christian and an unconverted heathen: the question of how the grace of God reaches the individual is not discussed, nor was any opinion dealing with this subject included among the heresies of Bardaisan. The main question actually in dispute between Bardaisan and Awida was whether such a thing as Free-will in man exists, and what was the sphere of its activity. It is a question still discussed, though I suppose the advocates of Free-will tend to become more diffident. What, then, is the argument upon which Bardaisan is not afraid to rely? Bardaisan's theory is that the sphere of Free-will is mainly restricted to the building up of the individual character, and his argument for the existence of this moral Free-will is that the Christian Faith produces in those who embrace it a corresponding change of character, a change that can be seen and known of all men. Can we, dare we, use that argument now? I do not propose to follow up the philosophical conclusions involved, if the facts be granted. I can only speak as a student of ancient history. What I wish to point out is that the victory which overcame the ancient world actually meant a change in the individual's life, and that it was the mark of a living faith to influence the conduct. Whatever may be the philosophical explanation, the member of the ancient Christian Church—Bardaisan the heretic, as much as Justin Martyr—really felt within him a new and constraining force. That force was not possessed, or not possessed to anything like the same extent, by the opponents and rivals of Christianity. Half the jealousy with which the official world regarded the Church was due to the consciousness that the source from which the Church drew its life and its force lay outside and independent of the State. What gave Christianity this force is another question, but the early Christians were well aware of it, and we shall never understand the history of the rise of Christianity unless we remember its existence. That inward force is the real, indispensable Note of the true Church: the future will belong to the Church only if she is able to supply the constraining power over individual conduct, to the evident effects of which Bardaisan was not afraid to appeal.

EDESSA.
View looking N.N.W.

[To face p. 193.

LECTURE VI

THE ACTS OF JUDAS THOMAS AND THE HYMN OF THE SOUL

The art of telling a tale is perhaps the most wonderful of all human inventions, and the East has ever been famous for story-telling. We shall therefore not be surprised to find that the most striking and original piece of Syriac Literature is a Novel. By a curious chance, which I suspect would prove to be, if we knew more, less a chance than an intimate literary connexion, this Novel contains within it an independent Poem which itself is the most beautiful production not of Syriac Literature only, but I venture to assert of all the literary activity of the early Church. The Novel is the *Acts of Judas Thomas*, the Apostle of India: the Poem is known to modern scholars as the *Hymn of the Soul*.

The work called the Acts of Thomas in one form or another has long been familiar to hagiographers and ecclesiologists. When you see a stained glass window with S. Thomas depicted in it, he will probably be represented with a spear in his hand. That is because according to these Acts the apostle was martyred with spears. In a sense, therefore, the story of S. Thomas is no new discovery. But it is only lately that it has been recovered in approximately its original form, and it is only lately that it has been recognised as a story which is Syriac in origin. Even now the work is familiar only to professed scholars: Wright's English translation is out of print, and the outside world knows very little of a tale that can challenge comparison with the *Pilgrim's Progress*.

It will be convenient, before entering more into detail about the various problems suggested by the *Acts of Thomas*, to give a short abstract of the story which forms the framework of the book.[1]

I. At the beginning we are told how the Twelve Apostles divided the countries of the earth among themselves by lot, and that the lot which fell to Judas Thomas—Judas the Twin —was India. But Judas Thomas did not wish to go and preach to the Indians, so our Lord appeared to an Indian merchant named Ḥabbân, a servant of King Gundaphar, and sold Thomas to him as a slave. Thomas and Ḥabbân go off by sea and disembark at the town of Sandarûk. Here they

---

[1] A complete English Translation is given in Wright's *Apocryphal Acts*, vol. ii, pp. 146-298. What is given here is taken mainly from my own book *Early Christianity outside the Roman Empire*, p. 64 ff.

find that the King of the place is making a great feast to celebrate his only daughter's marriage, and they go in with the rest to the public feast. At the feast Thomas sings a curious Hymn. He also prophecies the violent death of one of the guests who had behaved rudely to him, an event which comes to pass that very night. The King hears of this and forces Thomas to go in and pray over the bride; he does so and then departs. But when the bride and bridegroom are alone our Lord appears to them in the likeness of Thomas and persuades them both to a life of virginity. In the end the King also is converted, and the young people join S. Thomas in India.

II. Meanwhile Thomas and Ḥabbân had gone on to King Gundaphar in India, and Thomas is set to build a palace for the King. To this story, which forms a complete episode by itself, we shall return later.

III. After the palace-building episode Judas Thomas brings back to life a youth who had been killed by a devil in the form of a black snake. In this story, as in some of the others, the prayers and exhortations of Thomas are given at considerable length, so that a mere description of the action by no means exhausts the interest of the story.

IV. Next an ass's colt, of the stock that served Balaam the prophet, comes and speaks and directs the apostle to a certain city. At the gate of the city the colt falls down and dies, having performed its mission.

V. In the city Thomas delivers a beautiful woman from the attacks of a devil. The woman is baptized and she receives the Communion.

VI. During the ceremony a young man's hand withers and he confesses that he had killed a woman who would not live a life of virginity with him. On his repentance he brings Judas Thomas to the dead woman's body, and at his prayer she is restored to life. She then describes the torments of the unchaste that she had seen in hell, and the incident closes with an exhortation from the apostle.

VII. After these things, while the Apostle is preaching in India, the General of King Mazdai, named Sîfûr, comes beseeching him to free his wife and daughter from evil and lascivious devils. Judas Thomas leaves his converts under the care of the deacon Xanthippus and goes with the General. On the way the horses of their chariot break down, but four wild asses come up to be harnessed in their stead, and with their help the devils are driven out and the women healed.

VIII. Soon after this a noble lady, by name Mygdonia, the wife of Kârîsh, a kinsman of King Mazdai, is converted by Judas Thomas to the life of virginity. Kârîsh is in despair; and when his personal influence fails to move Mygdonia, he goes and complains to the King, by whose orders Thomas is arrested at the house of Sîfûr the General. The apostle is scourged and sent to prison, where he sings that *Hymn* to which we shall return further on. Mygdonia remains firm and secretly visits Thomas in the prison with her nurse Narqia: there he baptizes them and celebrates the Eucharist. In the meanwhile King Mazdai and Kârîsh, who regard the conversion of Mygdonia as due to magic and enchantment, agree to let Thomas go if he will tell her to be as she was before. Thomas warns them that it will be useless, and that neither his persuasion nor tortures would change her new spirit. This is proved to be the case, for Mygdonia refuses to listen to the Apostle when he pretends to counsel her to go back to her husband. After this Thomas returns to the house of Sîfûr the General and baptizes him and his family, and gives them also the Eucharist: at the same time Mygdonia converts Tertia, the wife of King Mazdai. Mazdai now becomes seriously angry and drags Thomas off to prison again, but on the way he converts Wîzân, the King's son. In the prison the Apostle makes his final address, beginning with the Lord's Prayer, which is quoted in full. Manashar, Wîzân's wife (who has just been healed of a long sickness by our Lord Himself, who appeared to her in the form of a youth), joins them in the prison, and the Apostle baptizes Wîzân,

Manashar, and Tertia. In the morning Thomas is brought out and condemned to death by the King: he is taken outside the town and after a short prayer is speared by four soldiers. Before his death he had ordained Sîfûr and Wîzân, and the converts continue in the faith after having been encouraged by a vision of the ascended Judas Thomas.

The bones of the Apostle were secretly taken away to the "West" by one of the brethren, but a long time afterwards the dust from the grave charms away a devil from one of King Mazdai's sons, whereupon the King also believes and prays Sîfûr and the brethren for forgiveness.

Such is the tale of S. Thomas. It is very likely that some of the details of the legend are older than the book of *Acts*, of which I have just given a short summary. The reputed bones of Thomas the Apostle were preserved at Edessa, at least from the middle of the fourth century onwards, and some story of their adventures had doubtless grown up round the shrine.

One of the most curious features of the tale has lately been investigated by Dr Rendel Harris in his brilliant study of the influence of the Heavenly Twins on Christian legend.[1] We all know that Thomas means "twin," and the Syriac tradition had it that the name of the apostle whom we call Thomas was Judas the Twin. Consequently the earliest Syriac text of the Gospels calls that Judas who was not Iscariot (Joh. xiv 22) by the same name

---
[1] J. R. Harris, *The Dioscuri in the Christian Legends*, pp. 20-41.

as the hero of our tale, *viz.* Judas Thomas. The surprising circumstance is that throughout these *Acts* this Judas Thomas, the Apostle, is assumed to be the twin-brother of our Lord Himself. Not only do men and women in these *Acts* mistake the one for the other, but the very devils and wild beasts salute the Apostle as "Twin of the Messiah."[1] No wonder that some of our MSS. have obliterated the title!

It was this strange title and the ideas underlying it that Dr Harris investigated, and I venture to think we may accept his main conclusion, which is that the Christian figures of our Lord and S. Thomas have displaced a heathen cult of Twins, one mortal and the other immortal, like Castor and Pollux, like the Evening Star that sets and disappears and the Morning Star that remains in the sky until the perfect day has dawned. Dr Harris goes on to find the genesis of several curious features in the story of S. Thomas as told in the *Acta Thomae*. For instance, the hypothesis that the Christian hero has taken over the attributes of the Dioscuri, the Great Twin Brethren, may be used to explain why the apostle is represented as a stone-cutter as well as a carpenter,

---
[1] *Wright* 197, 208 (E. Transl., pp. 170, 180).

and why he appears in the legend as a tamer of wild asses. In this connexion it is worth notice that in a passage from the Bardesanian Dialogue on Fate, quoted in the previous Lecture (see p. 170), a passage which is closely imitated in the Acts of Thomas also, certain arts are mentioned in which Christians are not expected as Christians to be proficient, *viz.* stone-cutting, building, and navigation; these very arts are included among the traditional activities of the Dioscuri. But there must at present remain much that is doubtful and much that is still obscure in this fascinating line of study.[1]

With the *Acts of Thomas*, as with all good literature, it is better to let the book speak for itself. I shall therefore tell you the tale of how Judas Thomas the Apostle came into India and built a Palace for the King in Heaven.[2]

"And when Judas had entered into the realm of India with the merchant Ḥâbban, Ḥâbban went to salute Gundaphar the King of India, and he told him of the artificer whom he had brought for him. And the King was very glad, and ordered Judas to come into his presence. And the King said to him: 'What art dost thou know to practise?' Judas

---

[1] Especially hazardous is Dr Harris's attempt to read the mutilated Inscription on one of the two great Columns at Edessa as a dedication to the constellation *Gemini*. The two great Columns are shown in the frontispiece to this volume, but I could not obtain a photograph of the inscription.

[2] Wright's *Apocryphal Acts*, English Translation, pp. 159-165.

saith to him: 'I am a carpenter, the servant of a carpenter and architect.' He saith to him: 'What dost thou know how to make?' Judas saith to him: 'In wood I know how to make yokes and ploughs and ox-goads, and oars for barges and ferry-boats and masts for ships; and in hewn stone, tombstones and monuments and palaces for Kings.' The King saith to Judas: 'And I want such an artificer.' The King saith to him: 'Wilt thou build me a palace?' Judas saith to him: 'I will build it and finish it, for I am come to work at building and carpentering.'

"And he took him and went outside the gate of the city, and was talking with him about the constructing of the palace, and about its foundations how they should be laid. And when he had reached the place where the King wished him to build a palace for him, he said to Judas: 'Here I wish you to build for me a palace.' Judas saith to him: 'Yes, for this is a place which is suitable for it.' Now it was of this sort; it was a meadow, and there was plenty of water near it. The King saith to him: 'Begin to build here.' Judas saith to him: 'Now I cannot build at this time.' The King saith to him: 'And at what time wilt thou be able to build?' Judas saith: 'I will begin in Autumn and I will finish in Spring.' The King saith to him: 'All buildings are built in summer; and dost thou build in winter?' Judas saith to him: 'Thus only is it possible for the palace to be built.' The King saith to him: 'Well then, trace it out for me that I may see it, because it is a long time before I shall come hither.' And Judas came and took a cane and began to measure; and he left doors towards the east for light, and windows toward the west for air, and they made the bake-house to the South, and the water-pipes for the service of the house to the North. The King saith to him: 'Verily thou art a good artificer and worthy to serve a King.' And he left a large sum of money and departed from him, and more silver and gold he was sending to him from time to time.

"But Judas was going about in the villages and in the cities, and was ministering to the poor and was making the afflicted comfortable, and he was saying: 'What is the King's to the Kings shall be given, and rest there shall be for many.'

"And after a long time the King despatched messengers to Judas and sent to him thus: 'Send me word what thou hast done and what I shall send thee.' And Judas sent him word: 'The palace is built, but the roof is wanting to it.' Then the King sent to Judas silver and gold, and sent him word: 'Let the palace be roofed.' And the Apostle was glorifying our Lord and saying: 'I thank Thee Lord, who didst die that Thou mightest give me life; and who didst sell me that I might be the liberator of many.' And he did not cease to teach and to relieve those who were afflicted, saying: 'May your Lord give you rest, to whom alone is the glory; for He is the nourisher of the orphans and the provider of the widows, and He ministers unto all those who are afflicted.'

"And when the King came to the city, he was asking every one of his friends about the palace which Judas had built for him; but they say unto him: 'There is no palace built, nor has he done anything else but going about the cities and the villages and giving to the poor and teaching them the new God, and also healing the sick and driving out demons and doing many like things; and we declare that he is a sorcerer, but his compassion and his healing, which was done without recompense, and his asceticism and his piety declare about him that either he is a Magian or an Apostle of the new God. For he fasts much and prays much and eats bread and salt and drinks water and wears one garment, and takes nothing from any man for himself, and whatever he has he gives to others.' And when the King heard these things, he smote his face with his hands and was shaking his head.

"And he sent and called Judas and the merchant who had bought him, and said to him: 'Hast thou built me the palace?' Judas saith to him: 'I have built thee the palace.'

The King saith to him: 'When can we go and look at it?' Judas saith to him: 'Thou canst not see it now, but when thou hast departed from this world.' Then the King became furious in his anger, and commanded that Thomas and the merchant who had brought him should go in bonds to prison, till he could question him about his doings, to whom he had given the treasure, and then destroy him. But Judas went rejoicing and said to the merchant: 'Fear not, but only believe, and thou shalt be freed from this world, and shalt receive everlasting life in the world to come.'

"And the King was considering by what death he should kill Judas and the merchant; and he took the resolution that he would flay him alive and burn him with the merchant his companion. And in that very night the King's brother, whose name was Gad, was taken ill through grief and through the imposition which had been practised on the King. And he sent and called the King and said to him: 'My brother, I commend unto thee my house and my children, for I am grieved and am dying because of the imposition that hath been practised upon thee. If thou dost not punish that sorcerer, thou wilt not let my soul be at peace in Sheol.' The King saith to him: 'The whole night I have been considering how I should kill him, and I have resolved to flay him alive and burn him.' Then the King's brother said to him: 'And if there be anything worse than this, do it to him; and I give thee charge of my house and my children.'

"And when he had said these things, his soul left him. And the King was grieved for his brother, because he loved him much, and he was intending to bury him in a splendid grave. But when the soul of Gad, the King's brother, had left him, angels took it and bore it up to heaven; and they were showing it each place in succession, to see in which of them it wished to be. Then, when they came to the palace which Judas had built for the King, his brother saw it and said to the angels: 'I beg of you, my lords, let me dwell in one of the lower chambers of this palace.' The angels say to him:

'Thou canst not dwell in this palace.' He saith to them: 'Wherefore?' They say to him: 'This palace is the one which the Christian hath built for thy brother.' Then he said to them: 'I beg of you, my lords, let me go, that I may go and buy of him this palace; for my brother doth not understand the matter and he will sell it to me.'

"Then the angels let go the soul of Gad. And as his body was being enshrouded, his soul came into him, and he said to those who were standing before him: 'Call my brother to me that I may make of him one request.' Then they sent word to the King: 'Thy brother is come to life.' And the King sprang up from his place and went into the house of his brother with a number of people. And when he had gone in beside the bed, he was astounded and unable to speak with him. His brother saith to him: 'I know, my brother, that if a man had asked thee for the half of thy kingdom thou wouldst have given it for my sake. And now I beg of thee that thou sell me that at which thou hast laboured.' The King saith to him: 'Tell me, what shall I sell thee?' He saith to him: 'Swear unto me.' And he sware unto him that he would grant him whatever he asked of all that he had. He saith to him: 'Sell me the palace which thou hast in heaven.' The King saith to him: 'Who hath given me a palace in heaven?' His brother saith to him: 'That which the Christian hath built for thee.' Then the King understood, and he said to his brother: 'That I cannot sell to thee; but I pray and beg of God that I may enter into it and receive it, and may be worthy to be among its inhabitants. And thou, if thou dost really wish to buy thyself a palace, this architect will build one for thee which will be better than that of mine.' And the King sent and brought out Judas and the merchant who was imprisoned with him, and said to him: 'I beg of thee as a man who begs a minister of God, that thou wouldst pray for me, and beg for me from the God that thou worshippest, that He would forgive me what I have done unto thee, and that he would make me worthy to enter into the palace which thou hast built for me, and that I may become a worshipper of this God whom thou preachest.'"

Thus the King and his brother were converted, and presently they were baptized by Judas Thomas and admitted to Christian Communion.

I have quoted you this story almost in full, partly for its own sake, partly that you may have an opportunity of comparing what is undoubtedly an integral part of the Acts of Thomas with the poem imbedded in these Acts which we call the *Hymn of the Soul*.

The real interest of the *Acts of Thomas* to the student of Eastern Christianity does not lie in the adventures of the Apostle, but in his prayers and sermons, in the doctrine that he teaches. These are not mere embellishments of the narrative, but the very essence of the book. What the author wishes us to give our earnest attention is the Gospel of Virginity and Poverty and its effect on the soul. As to the intense seriousness of the work there can be no doubt at all: no early Christian writer, orthodox or heterodox, would quote the Lord's Prayer in full merely for ornament.

In treating this book of Apocryphal Acts as a work Syriac in origin and not a translation from the Greek, I have ventured to assume a result which I have endeavoured elsewhere to prove.[1] Many of the most cogent arguments depend on critical details and the niceties of Syriac grammar, the discussion of which would be quite out of place in Lectures such as these. It will be sufficient therefore to say that the Syriac origin of the *Acts of Thomas* is now maintained by nearly every Syriac scholar, from my friend Dr Nöldeke of Strassburg downwards. But apart from philological argument we may point out in passing that the whole framework of the tale belongs to the countries washed by the Euphrates and the Tigris. The proper names are such as would occur to a Syriac-speaking Christian, but they could hardly have been invented by a Greek, It is to Justi's *Iranisches Namenbuch* and not to Pape's *Griechische Eigennamen* that we have to look for their elucidation. Mazdai, Wêzân, Manashar, are good old-Persian names. Mygdonia is called after the river of Nisibis, just as the Edessan Bardaisan was called after the river of Edessa. It is surely significant that in the only ancient Roman deed of sale of a slave from Mesopotamia which has found its way into a modern library

---

[1] See *Journal of Theological Studies*, i 280-290, ii 429, iii 94; compare Bonnet's *Acta Philippi et Acta Thomae* (Leipzig, 1903), pp. xx ff.

the name of the slave is *Abbanes*, the same name as that of the merchant who bought Judas Thomas from Jesus Christ. Except Xanthippus the deacon and Tertia the queen there is not one European-sounding name among all the characters of the novel.[1]

I have designated the *Acts of Thomas* as unorthodox. This perhaps requires some justification. Judged by the ordinary Western standard it is in many ways heretical, but the standard of the early Syriac-speaking Church was that of Aphraates rather than that of Athanasius. Even in the matter of marriage and continence we cannot at once say that he is in absolute conflict with the teaching of his Church, for in prohibiting his baptized converts to marry, or to live as man and wife, he is doing no more than what Aphraates prohibited. We have already seen that the state of matrimony was not recognised as holy by early Syriac Christianity. Nor again does the unorthodoxy of these *Acts* rest entirely on the elements commonly recognised as "Gnostic."

---

[1] Dr Harris (*Dioscuri*, p. 27) suggests that this may have been a recognised name of one of the charioteers of the Heavenly Twins. Xanthippus is only mentioned in the Acts of Thomas (*Wright*, p. 204) as the person whom the Apostle leaves in charge when he goes away. Even so did King Ptolemy Euergetes: "Ciliciam autem amico suo Antiocho gubernandam tradidit et *Xanthippo* alteri duci *prouincias trans Euphraten*" (Jerome on Dan xi 9, quoted by E. R. Bevan, *House of Seleucus* i 189, note).

These consist of certain mystical and very imperfectly understood expressions in the prayers and invocations of S. Thomas. I do not wish to minimise the interest of these curious phrases; obscure as they are, they present unmistakeable points of contact with the equally obscure phrases of the Bardesanian hymns quoted by S. Ephraim. It is true, moreover, that some of these expressions have been removed from the Syriac text as preserved in the British Museum MS. used by Wright, and many more have been left out in the Sachan MS. at Berlin used by Bedjan, and so we find them only in the ancient Greek translation. But some at least of the queer phrases in the Greek are the result not of heterodox doctrine but of the ignorance or helplessness of the translator.

Yet I venture to think that the real heresy of the writer of the *Acts of Thomas* is not to be found in his cosmogony, but in his independence and the puritan recklessness of his attitude. From the moment that S. Thomas starts for India we hear no more of the other Apostles. He is absolutely independent of every one except his Lord. The word Church occurs only once and that by mistake. Uncatholic also is the want of interest in controversy against the Jews and against idolatry. Judas

Thomas does not bring forward unorthodox opinions about the old dispensation or the worship of heathen gods: he simply passes these things by with the turn of a phrase. Thus we read (E. Transl., p. 207) that God's will was spoken by the Prophets, but Israel did not obey because of their evil genius.[1] Again, the devils confess that they take pleasure in sacrifices of wine on the altars as well as in murder and adultery (E. Transl., p. 213).[2] But these are mere allusions by the way: it is not so much against the gods that S. Thomas preaches as against the evil nature in man. Contrast this with the elaborate polemic against the Jews in Aphraates, and the long sermons against idolatry in the *Doctrine of Addai*. So much indeed is it the rule that the "Acts" of martyrs should contain a testimony against the worship of idols that in the Latin version of the *Acta Thomae* there is an extended interpolation, telling how S. Thomas refused to worship the Sun-god when he was brought before King Mazdai.

The interest of the author of the *Acts of Thomas* lay in the workings of human nature,

---

[1] In the Syriac *yaṣr'hôn bîshâ*: cf. Deut xxxi 21 and the corresponding Jewish doctrines.

[2] See also Transl., p. 198.

not in the conflicting claims of rival religions—in a word, it lay in the conversion of individual souls rather than in the establishment of a Church. But to the Catholic writers from the very first the case was different. To them the Jewish question was vital, not so much for the sake of convincing the Jews of error as to establish their own position. There stood the Holy Oracles, the promises of God to His people—to whom did they apply? It was as essential for the early Church to establish her claim to be the true heir of the Covenants, as it is for the High Anglican of our day to make out a case for the apostolical succession of the English bishops. With the Gnostic, unless I am mistaken, the position of things was not quite the same. Early Christianity was a historical religion, proved by texts out of the Old Testament and by the events of the life of Jesus of Nazareth: Gnosticism, on the other hand, was more what we call natural religion, a philosophy. The philosophy might be illustrated from the Old Testament or the New, but it was really independent of the Bible. It was not the application of the old promises of God that troubled the author of the *Acts of Thomas* but the aimlessness of men's lives, which to him appeared to be filled with care and sorrow about that which must quickly pass away for ever.

In the conception of the Church—that is, the organised body of believers,—as a thing in itself to be worked for and fostered, lies the true point of difference between Catholicism and Gnosticism, between Aphraates and the *Acts of Thomas*. To the convert of Judas Thomas there was literally nothing left on this earth to live for. "Would that the days passed swiftly over me, and that all the hours were one," says Mygdonia, "that I might go forth from this world; and go and see that Beautiful One the tale of Whom I have heard,[1] that Living One and Giver of life to those who have believed in Him, where there is neither day nor night, and no darkness but light, and neither good nor bad, nor rich nor poor, neither male nor female, nor slaves nor freemen, nor any proud and uplifted over those who are humble."[2] The old civilisation was doomed, but this religious Nihilism puts nothing in its place. To the orthodox Christian, on the other hand, the Church stood like Aaron between the dead and the living, as a middle term between the things of the next world and

---

[1] *Sic*: Wright's text is here supported by the ancient Sinai fragments.
[2] *Wright*, Transl., p. 265.

of this. It was the Body of Christ and therefore eternal; something worth living for and working for. Yet it was in the world as much as the Empire itself. The idea of the Church thus formed an invaluable fixed point, round which a new civilisation could slowly crystallise.

The *Acts of Thomas* tell us that the Apostle was arrested at the house of Sîfûr after the conversion of Mygdonia and thrown into prison by the order of King Mazdai. In the prison, like Paul and Silas at Philippi, he sings a Hymn; but the Hymn which he is said to have sung is not in the least like anything we should have expected to find. And indeed, although this Hymn is contained in the ancient Greek versions so happily discovered by Professor Bonnet, as well as in the Syriac MS. used by Dr Wright, it is universally agreed that it is a distinct independent work.[1] It had originally nothing to do with the *Acts of Thomas*, and most people think that it has only been inserted in

---

[1] The original Syriac text of the Hymn is given in Wright's *Apocryphal Acts* i 274-279 (E. Transl., pp. 238-245); the Greek translation is edited in M. Bonnet's *Acta Thomae* (ed. of 1903), pp. 219-224, and see *Analecta Bollandiana* xx 159-164.

its present position by an ancient editor.[1] That it is a Syriac composition is clear, not only from the style, but also from the fact that it is written in metre. It is arranged in lines of twelve syllables each, divided by a pause which breaks up the line into two half-verses of six and six or five and seven syllables respectively, and further the twelve-syllable lines seem to me to fall into stanzas of five lines each. In the translation which I am about to read to you, I have tried to represent each of the twelve-syllable lines of the Syriac by an English Hexameter.

The use of this metre is the less inappropriate as the poem is cast in narrative form. We call it the *Hymn of the Soul*, but it is not so much a Hymn as a short Epic, telling the tale of the Prince who went down to Egypt to fetch the Serpent-guarded Pearl. As we travel with the hero we are brought into unfamiliar regions. The home of the Prince is the old Parthian Empire, roughly corresponding to

---

[1] I cannot help expressing a private opinion that the Hymn was inserted by the author of the *Acts* himself, just as he used the Lord's Prayer in a later prayer of Judas Thomas. That the Hymn itself is independent of the *Acts of Thomas* is certain, but it is not so clear that the *Acts of Thomas* is independent of the Hymn. The great Hymn, in fact, may have become a part of the recognised teaching of the sect to which the author of the *Acts* belonged (cf. Ephraim's *Commentary* on 3 *Corinthians*, p. 119).

modern Persia. The King, his Father, lives either in Hyrcania near the southern shores of the Caspian Sea, or as it were in Rhages near Teheran. The wealth of the Kingdom is deposited in Elymais and the mountain sanctuaries of Atropatene (the modern Adherbaiján), or comes from over the mountains, from the unknown lands of India. With the tact of a poet the author does not mention the modern cities of Ctesiphon and Seleucia; to the Prince all the Euphrates Valley is the Land of Babylon, a foreign hostile region peopled with demons. Egypt also is far from being the land we all know so well, the granary of the Roman Empire; in our *Hymn* it is an unclean land, the land of magic and enchantment from which the Chosen People of old escaped, a land mysteriously situate beyond the sea. But between Babylon and the sea, where the hero strikes the plain on his way down from his native mountains, is the district of Maishán or Mesene, a friendly country to some extent under his Father's dominion. The only companion he can make in the hated land of Egypt appears to be a merchant from Maishán, a stranger there like himself; and on his return journey it is when he reaches Maishán that the dangers of the route come to an end.

Although the narrative is never once interrupted by preaching or philosophy, the general scope of the Allegory is clear. In the words of Nöldeke:[1] "We have here an ancient Gnostic hymn relating to the Soul, which is sent from its heavenly home to the earth, and there forgets both its origin and its mission until it is aroused by a revelation from on high; thereupon it performs the task assigned to it and returns to the upper regions, where it is re-united to the heavenly robe, its ideal counterpart, and enters the presence of the highest celestial Powers." Yet it may be worth while to point out that some of the details are not really so strange as they appear at first sight to us, who are accustomed to look at the theory of our Religion only through the spectacles of Greek Theology. The *King of Kings*, the *Queen of the East*, and the next in rank, the *Viceroy*, are the Father, Mother, and Brother of the Soul. They seem to correspond to the Father, the Holy Spirit, and the Son. This presentation was shocking to the Greek mind of the fourth century, but we have already seen that in Semitic languages *Spirit* or *Wind* is feminine, and that Aphraates himself does not scruple to call the Holy Spirit the Mother of

---

[1] Quoted in A. A. Bevan's *Hymn of the Soul*, p. 2.

a man—that Mother, in fact, whom the Scripture declares him to forsake when he marries a wife.[1]

The thought of the Heavenly Robe is perhaps even less familiar to us, though not to earlier Christian speculation. S. Paul (2 Cor. v 2) speaks of "earnestly desiring to be clothed upon with our house which is from heaven." That which S. Paul desired was no fixed "house" or "habitation," but a Heavenly Form. So here, too, the Robe is no article of clothing, but a Bright Form. The Syriac word means *The Bright* or *The Shining* thing. It is "put off" and "put on" by the Soul, and it "spreads itself out" like a garment; on the other hand, it is represented as assuming the appearance of the returning Prince and even as speaking with its Guardians. The word "body" is never used either of it or of the Soul, "stature" being used instead. I have kept *Robe* as the most satisfactory English equivalent for this Body Celestial.

Over the Robe is cast a Tunic of royal scarlet, and within dwells the true Soul. But when the time comes for the Soul to be born into this world, the Heavenly Vesture must be left behind in the presence of the Father.[2] There

---

[1] Wright's *Aphraates*, p. 354; see above, p. 89.

[2] Compare Matt. xviii 10, and see the illuminating Essay by Dr J. H. Moulton, called "It is his Angel" (*Journal of Theol. Studies*, iii 514-527).

it grows with the growth of the Soul on earth and suffers with its failures. At last the Soul has done its work here; it strips off for ever the unclean garment of the earthly body, and it meets once more its Heavenly Frame on its way back to the Father's Home.

There is reason to suppose that the Hymn was composed before the overthrow of the Parthian dynasty in 224 A.D. The whole machinery of the poem, so far as it does not belong to fairyland, is borrowed from the conditions of the Parthian empire. There is nothing to show that while their successors the Sasanians were in power the people of Roman Mesopotamia ever looked back to the hegemony of the Parthians as to an ideal or golden age, or indeed that the special features of Parthian rule and the political geography of the Parthian dominions were familiar at Edessa after that rule had passed away. Thus the composition of the Hymn falls within the lifetime of Bardaisan, and we may indulge the pleasing fancy that it was the work of Bardaisan himself or of his son Harmonius. You will find the question as adequately discussed as the paucity of the evidence allows in the Introduction which my friend Professor A. A. Bevan has prefixed to his edition of the Hymn. Professor Bevan concludes with words which I take this opportunity to quote:[1] "Whatever may be the ultimate verdict of scholars as to the exact date and authorship of this composition, it will always deserve careful study on account of the light which it throws upon one of the most remarkable phrases in the religious history of mankind. Gnosticism is here displayed to us not as it appeared to its enemies, not as a tissue of fantastic speculations, but as it was in reality, at least to some of its adherents, a new religion. Though the religious conceptions of the author are, in some respects, very closely akin to those of the early Christians, he nowhere refers directly to the New Testament, nor does he even allude to the historical facts on which Christianity is founded. Yet he does not speak doubtfully, as one feeling after truth; his convictions, such as they are, respecting the realities of the unseen world, rest upon what he believes to be a direct revelation, symbolised by the living letter which the King sealed with his right hand. Until this state of mind is understood, the nature of Oriental Gnosticism and of the struggle which it long maintained, against Paganism on the one side and traditional Christianity on the other, must remain a mystery."

---

[1] A. A. Bevan, *Hymn of the Soul*, p. 7 [Texts and Studies v 3].

And now we come to the *Hymn* itself:—

I

WHILE I was yet but a little child in the House of my Father,
Brought up in luxury, well content with the life of the Palace,
Far from the East, our home, my Parents sent me to travel,
And from the royal Hoard they prepared me a load for the journey,
Precious it was yet light, that alone I carried the burden.

II

Median gold it contained and silver from Atropatene,
Garnet and ruby from Hindostan and Bactrian agate,
Adamant harness was girded upon me stronger than iron;
But my Robe they took off wherewith their love had adorned me,
And the bright Tunic woven of scarlet and wrought to my stature.

III

For they decreed, and wrote on my heart that I should not forget it:
"If thou go down and bring from Egypt the Pearl, the unique one,
"Guarded there in the Sea that envelopes the loud-hissing Serpent,
"Thou shalt be clothed again with thy Robe and the Tunic of scarlet,
"And with thy Brother, the Prince, shalt thou inherit the Kingdom."

IV

So I quitted the East, two Guardians guiding me downwards,
Hard was the way for a child and a dangerous journey to travel,
Soon I had passed Maishán, the mart of the Eastern merchants,
Over the soil of Babylon then I hurried my footsteps,
And my companions left me within the borders of Egypt.

V

Straight to the Serpent I went and near him settled my dwelling,
Till he should slumber and sleep, and the Pearl I could snatch from his keeping,
I was alone, an exile under a foreign dominion,
None did I see of the free-born race of the Easterns,
Save one youth, a son of Maishán, who became my companion.

VI

He was my friend to whom I told the tale of my venture,
Warned him against the Egyptians and all their ways of uncleanness;
Yet in their dress I clothed myself to escape recognition,
Being afraid lest when they saw that I was a stranger
Come from afar for the Pearl, they would rouse the Serpent against me.

VII

It was from him perchance they learnt I was none of their kindred,
And in their guile they gave me to eat of their unclean dainties;
Thus I forgot my race and I served the King of the country,
Nay, I forgot the Pearl for which my parents had sent me,
While from their poisonous food I sank into slumber unconscious.

VIII

All that had chanced my Parents knew and they grieved for me sorely,
Through the land they proclaimed for all at our Gate to assemble—
Parthian Princes and Kings, and all the Eastern Chieftains—
There they devised an escape that I should not perish in Egypt,
Writing a letter signed in the name of each of the Chieftains.

IX

"From thy Father, the King of Kings,—from the Queen, thy Mother,—
"And from thy Brother,—to thee, our Son in Egypt, be greeting!
"Up and arise from sleep, and hear the words of our Letter!
"Thou art a son of Kings: by whom art thou held in bondage?
"Think of the Pearl for which thou wast sent to sojourn in Egypt.

X

"Think of thy shining Robe and remember thy glorious Tunic;
"These thou shalt wear when thy name is enrolled in the list of the heroes,
"And with thy Brother Viceroy thou shalt be in the Kingdom."
This was my Letter, sealed with the King's own Seal on the cover,
Lest it should fall in the hands of the fierce Babylonian demons.

XI

High it flew as the Eagle, King of the birds of the heaven,
Flew and alighted beside me, and spoke in the speech of my country,
Then at the sound of its tones I started and rose from my slumber;
Taking it up I kissed and broke the Seal that was on it,
And like the words engraved on my heart were the words of the Letter.

XII

So I remembered my Royal race and my free-born nature,
So I remembered the Pearl, for which they had sent me to Egypt,
And I began to charm the terrible loud-hissing Serpent:
Down he sank into sleep at the sound of the Name of my Father,
And at my Brother's Name, and the Name of the Queen, my Mother.

XIII

Then I seized the Pearl and homewards started to journey,
Leaving the unclean garb I had worn in Egypt behind me;
Straight for the East I set my course, to the light of the home-land,
And on the way in front I found the Letter that roused me—
Once it awakened me, now it became a Light to my pathway.

XIV

For with its silken folds it shone on the road I must travel,
And with its voice and leading cheered my hurrying footsteps,
Drawing me on in love across the perilous passage,
Till I had left the land of Babylon safely behind me
And I had reached Maishán, the sea-washed haven of merchants.

XV

What I had worn of old, my Robe with its Tunic of scarlet,
Thither my Parents sent from the far Hyrcanian mountains,
Brought by the hand of the faithful warders who had it in keeping;
I was a child when I left it nor could its fashion remember,
But when I looked, the Robe had received my form and my likeness.

XVI

It was myself that I saw before me as in a mirror;
Two in number we stood, yet only one in appearance,
Not less alike than the strange twin guardian figures
Bringing my Robe, each marked with the royal Escutcheon,
Servants both of the King whose troth restored me my Treasure.

XVII

Truly a royal Treasure appeared my Robe in its glory,
Gay it shone with beryl and gold, sardonyx and ruby,
Over its varied hues there flashed the colour of sapphire,
All its seams with stones of adamant firmly were fastened,
And upon all the King of Kings Himself was depicted.

XVIII

While I gazed it sprang into life as a sentient creature,
Even as if endowed with speech and hearing I saw it,
Then I heard the tones of its voice as it cried to the keepers:
"He, the Champion, he for whom I was reared by the Father—
"Hast thou not marked me, how my stature grew with his labours?"

XIX

All the while with a kingly mien my Robe was advancing,
Flowing towards me as if impatient with those who bore it;
I too longed for it, ran to it, grasped it, put it upon me,
Once again I was clothed in my Robe and adorned with its beauty,
And the bright many-hued Tunic again was gathered about me.

XX

Clad in the Robe I betook me up to the Gate of the Palace,
Bowing my head to the glorious Sign of my Father that sent it;
I had performed His behest and He had fulfilled what He promised,
So in the Satraps' Court I joined the throng of the Chieftains—
He with favour received me and near Him I dwell in the Kingdom.

Such is the *Hymn of the Soul*. Our MS. adds a fragment of yet another stanza, but the faulty metre warns us that the text has been ill preserved. It shows us however that the Prince who has returned to his Home looks forward yet to a great Day, when he will present his Pearl before the King of Kings, his Father. In that day, to change the imagery into S. Paul's more familiar language, God will be all in all.

It is difficult for our distant age and Western civilisation to judge the great Hymn. We live, so to speak, in the unclean land of Egypt, and we cannot see the light of the East or hear the words of the winged Letter. We are all full of schemes for improving the world in which we actually find ourselves, and are very sceptical of a teaching which tells us that we are only strangers and sojourners and that our true home is elsewhere. This is natural enough in an age like ours, when every decennium marks some new discovery of the nature and action of the wonderful forces around us which condition our present existence. No one longs for next year in the early summer, much less in the spring. The age of the author of the *Hymn* and of the author of the *Acts of Thomas* was very different from that in which we live. They lived in a world that was beginning to wear out, a *Civitas Mundi* that had passed its prime. All that was best in the old civilisation in Science, in Art, in Literature, in Philosophy, in all that goes to make up the pageant of human life, had already been done, and the world needed re-birth.

Thus it came to pass that to the early Christian thinkers the life we live here seemed only valuable for that which we may take away with us when we quit it: the Merchant's goods were worth nothing in comparison with the Pearl of great price. Happiness, satisfaction, rest, these belonged according to their teaching altogether to the other life. "As long as we are in the world," says S. Thomas to his converts, "we are unable to speak about that which all the believers in God are going to receive. For if we say that He hath given us Light, we mention something which we have seen; and if we say that He hath given us Wealth, we mention something that is in the world; and if we speak of Clothing, we mention something that nobles wear; and if we speak of dainty Meats, we mention something against which we are warned; and if we speak of this temporary Rest, a chastisement is appointed for it. But we speak of God and of our Lord Jesus, and of Angels and Watchers and Holy Ones, and of the New World, and of the incorruptible food of the Tree of Life, and of the draught of the Water of Life; of what Eye hath not seen, nor Ear heard, nor hath it entered into the Heart of man to conceive, what God hath prepared from of old for those who love Him."

It was the hope of this that sent the Saints of Eastern Christianity into the desert, that sent Simeon Stylites to his pillar, that induced many a nameless disciple to cut himself off from all that the State and the Family had to offer. It is not for us to blame them. Let us rather be thankful that our lot has been cast in an environment where the work immediately before us is great and worthy enough to absorb the energies of the most generously endowed. Our business, no doubt, is to work while it is called to-day; the time perhaps will come to our civilisation also, when the night falls and no man can work, but only dream of a day that is to be.

NOTE ON THE HYMN OF THE SOUL.

In view of the many difficulties which the original Syriac offers both in text and in interpretation, it may be of interest to subjoin the comment on it made by Niceta, Archbishop of Thessalonica, who published a Greek Epitome of the *Acts of Thomas* which has been unearthed by Professor Bonnet. The date when this Niceta flourished is uncertain, but it must have been before the middle of the eleventh century. After giving a paraphrase of the *Hymn*, Niceta says (*Analecta Bollandiana* xx 163) : "Thus, if I have rightly gauged the meaning of these parabolic words, the inspired Apostle clearly indicates in his description the fair origin of our race in the image of God, the incorruptible wealth of graces thence derived, the spiritual armour wherewith we are furnished for the fight against those who are spiritually called Egyptians and against the Old Serpent their leader and champion. We see their plots, their wiles, their charms, the inevitable fall of those who trust in them, the consequent waste of divine wealth, the lingering taint of sins, shadowed forth in the poem by sleep and torpor ; then the compassion from on high, the help afforded by the Holy Scriptures as if by a letter, after the arrival of which comes the turn, the awakening, the enlightenment through baptism, whereby we recover the precious Pearl. And in addition to all this we see the rejoicing which our God and Father and the Divine Powers around Him make at the return and the recall of them that have fallen, and finally the safe arrival of those eternal rewards which God has prepared for those that wholly turn unto Him. Strengthening by these words the timid and doubtful disposition of our souls and teaching us how by means of them we are to lead a new life, dead as we have become in sins, the Apostle Thomas left an eternal consolation not only for those then in the prison but also for all faint-hearted souls throughout the ages."

It is worth noticing that Niceta does not doubt that the doctrine of the *Hymn* is orthodox. In fact, the view that it is anything else than a Christian document is the conjecture of modern scholars.